"In this scholarly and accessible work, Dr. John Bergsma not only offers us a thorough walk-through of the biblical roots of the priesthood, he also reminds us of two essential points: we are all created for worship and we as disciples of Jesus have a mission in the world that is increasingly urgent given all that is going on around us."

FR. JOHN RICCARDO
*Executive Director, Acts XXIX*

"Dr. John Bergsma has done it again. He has taken something that seems very common (the priesthood) but whose deep meaning often goes unexplored and he has told us in easy-to-understand terms how very uncommon it really is. Adam as a priest, creation as a liturgical act, Jesus' 'supercharged' words at the Last Supper—if you think you know what a priest is, be prepared to have your mind blown."

DREW MARIANI
*Host, The Drew Mariani Show, Relevant Radio*

"With characteristic clarity and depth, John Bergsma identifies and unpacks the Scriptural foundations of the ministerial priesthood. Far from human or ecclesiastical 'invention,' it is Jesus himself who intended it, fulfilling in himself the types which prefigured it, and instituting a new priesthood in his very person. This volume makes clear that any account of the relationship between the royal priesthood of the baptized and the ministerial priesthood which views them 'competitively' fails in understanding them both. Readers, lay and ordained alike, will benefit from Dr. Bergsma's lucid analysis and a scholarship which is placed clearly at the service of the Gospel."

MSGR. MICHAEL HEINTZ, PhD

*Dean, Mount St. Mary's Seminary*

"All too many theologies of the priesthood fail to offer a deep exploration of its biblical foundations. In this fine work, Professor Bergsma provides much more than a simple apologetic; his sweeping tour from Eden to the New Jerusalem illustrates how a priestly identity is woven into the biblical anthropology of the people of Israel and the disciples of Jesus Christ. This work will significantly enrich one's appreciation for the need and function of the ordained priesthood, while at the same time deepening the understanding of the mission and responsibility of the common priesthood of the baptized. While easily accessible to any serious reader, one important audience of this work will be seminarians and priests, who will be drawn deeper into the biblical spiritual roots of their vocation and identity."

FR. JOHN KARTJE

*Rector/President, University of Saint Mary of the Lake*

# JESUS *and the* OLD TESTAMENT ROOTS *of the* PRIESTHOOD

# JESUS *and the*
# OLD TESTAMENT ROOTS
## *of the* PRIESTHOOD

## JOHN BERGSMA

EMMAUS
ROAD
PUBLISHING

Steubenville, Ohio
www.emmausroad.org

Emmaus Road Publishing
1468 Parkview Circle
Steubenville, Ohio 43952

©2021 John Bergsma
All rights reserved. Published 2021.
Printed in the United States of America.

Library of Congress Control Number: 2020945121
978-1-64585-073-1 (hardcover) / 978-1-64585-074-8 (paperback) /
978-1-64585-075-5 (ebook)

Cover design and layout by Emily Demary
Cover image: *The Last Supper*, Philippe de Champaigne, 1652,
The Louvre, Paris, France

# TABLE OF CONTENTS

INTRODUCTION..........1

CHAPTER 1..............7
The Priesthood from Adam to Abraham

CHAPTER 2.............45
The Priesthood from Isaac to the Exile

CHAPTER 3.............77
The Priesthood in the New Testament

CHAPTER 4...........137
The Scrolls, Celibacy, and Holy Orders

EPILOGUE .............161

# INTRODUCTION

I grew up in a Christian tradition vigorously opposed to calling their clergy "priests." We were doctrinally committed to the view that the only priesthood in the New Covenant was the common priesthood of the faithful: every baptized believer shared in Christ's priesthood (Rev 1:6) and was called to "present [their] bodies as a living sacrifice" to God (Rom 12:1). Of course, in a situation where everyone is a priest, it is the same in practice as no one being a priest. We denied that there was any difference in state or character between believers—no one was spiritually set aside to God or consecrated as a sacred person within the Church. The clerical role was (at least theoretically) merely functional rather than ontological. That is, it merely concerned what one did, not who one was. Our preachers, pastors, or ministers—the terms could be used interchangeably—were, in theory, merely men who led worship and preached because someone had to do it. And anyone else who happened to have the requisite gifts could do the same things if they so wished. In practice, however, we did tend to revere our clergy, and the older generation still referred to the minister as the "*Domine*," Latin for "Lord"!

Of course, I did grow up surrounded by many Catholics, as my father was a military chaplain. Upon discovering that my dad was a cleric, I would have to correct the inevitable response: "So your dad is a priest?" or "You mean your father is a Father?" No, I would explain, he is not a priest, except in the sense that all of us are baptized into Christ's priesthood. And no, he is not a "Father" in a clerical sense, because Jesus says clearly, "call no man your father on earth" (Matt 23:9).

The story of how I grew up to be a minister myself but then was dragged kicking, if not screaming, into the Catholic Church by the inexorable logic of the Scriptures and the early Church Fathers has been told in a different book and in various talks. Suffice it to say that a good Catholic friend got me to read the apostolic fathers while I was in my doctoral program in Scripture, and what I found in them flipped my whole view of Church history and the development of Christian doctrine upside down, with the result that gravity then pulled me into the Church.

Fast-forward several years, and Pope Emeritus Benedict XVI declares a "Year of the Priest." A local parish invites me to teach some sessions of their adult education class, and suggests "Priesthood in the Bible" as a topic, in keeping with the theme of the holy year. I had come around almost to the opposite place from my childhood in terms of my understanding of priesthood in Scripture. I grew up suspicious of priesthood in Scripture, although I had never gone in for the German liberal Protestant reading of the Old Testament that isolated all the priestly and liturgical material and assigned it to a post-exilic (i.e., after 537 BC) author or authors of the so-called "Priestly School" (typically just "P" for scholars). Even as a Protestant, I had a strong suspicion that this whole reading of the Old Testament, especially the Pentateuch, was a retrojection of Lutheran or post-Lutheran antagonism for the *Catholic* priesthood onto the Old Testament's *Israelite* priesthood. Everything associated with priests was categorized as dull, pedantic, lifeless, legalistic, ossified, etc. They downplayed the fact that several charismatic (in the general sense) personalities of the Old Testament were priests or Levites themselves.

I rejected that critical view stemming from nineteenth-century scholarship, but still did not appreciate the role of the priest in the Bible. But now, it was all different: from Adam in the Garden of Eden to the "priests of God and of Christ" (Rev 20:6) at the end of the Book of Revelation, I could see priesthood as a major thread holding together the biblical storyline. In a sense, the story of salvation was an account of the gift of priesthood to Adam, his loss of it in the Fall, and the long process of restoring his descendants to a priestly status over the centuries, culminating in Christ.

That's the story that I want to recount in this book. I still believe, as I did in my youth, that we are all baptized into Christ's priesthood: this is good Catholic doctrine. However, I also now appreciate with ever greater clarity that Jesus *did* intend for there to be a ministerial priesthood in the New Covenant: an order of men succeeding from the Apostles that would perform for God's people the usual roles assigned to priests: leading worship, offering sacrifice, interpreting God's law for daily life, and mediating the forgiveness of sins, to mention a few. I offer this book—which began as some informal parish talks and still has that conversational style—to all Catholics who would like to understand and deepen their faith and better practice their own "royal priesthood." But I also offer it in a particular way to seminarians and priests at a time in which priestly identity is under attack, and it is more necessary than ever to re-ground the doctrine of Holy Orders in divine Revelation itself. It has given me great satisfaction over the years to present some of this material at priests' retreats, conferences, and convocations around the country and observe an almost visible surge of energy that results as some of the most self-giving but overworked men in all of society realize once again both the responsibility and the privilege to which God has called them. The harvest is ripe; let us pray to the Lord of the harvest to send many more workers into his field (Matt 9:37–38).

# CHAPTER 1

# THE PRIESTHOOD FROM ADAM TO ABRAHAM

## IS THE PRIESTHOOD BIBLICAL?

While our first inclination is to say yes, we would not have to go very far to find people who would disagree. Many of our Protestant brothers and sisters will take issue with this, noting there's nothing in the New Testament explicitly talking about having priests in the Church. And if you point out that there's a priesthood in the Old Testament, they are likely to argue that this was a feature of the Old Covenant that was undone by Christ. The Catholic Church—insofar as we continue to have a priesthood—is living according to the Old Covenant rather than the New. How do we respond to that?

To rephrase the question: Is the practice of the Church based in Scripture or not? To adequately address that question, we need to journey through Scripture for a rich understanding of what the priesthood is all about. Let's begin with Adam in the Garden.

## THE PRIESTHOOD OF ADAM

Everyone knows that Moses' older brother Aaron was the first to hold the priesthood in the history of Israel. But when we look a little more closely, we can see that the idea of the priesthood reaches back to the very beginnings of Scripture. In fact, Adam himself enjoyed a certain kind of priesthood. It's not very explicit, but if we read Scripture carefully and are attuned to the subtle meanings of some of the words, we can recognize an implicit priestly role that Adam enjoyed.

The key text for our purposes is Genesis 2:15. The Revised Standard Version translates it this way: "The Lord God took the man and put him in the Garden of Eden to till it and to keep it." Notice the words "till" and "keep"; the translators have taken the meaning of the Hebrew and given it a horticultural spin, which makes a certain amount of sense because Adam is going into a Garden. A more literal translation of the Hebrew, however, would be "work" and "guard." Adam is put into the Garden to work it and to guard it. That's interesting.

These two words, *work* and *guard*, actually don't occur as a pair very often in Scripture. In fact, the next place that we find these two verbs being used together in the

Pentateuch (or the books of Moses) is several biblical books later, in Numbers. There, the Lord speaks to Moses about the Levites, who had been chosen as a priestly tribe:

> Bring the tribe of Levi near, and set them before Aaron the priest, that they may minister to him. They shall perform duties for him and for the whole congregation before the tent of meeting, as they minister at the tabernacle. (Num 3:6–7)

Again, translated literally, the Levites are told that "they shall *guard* the things to be *guarded*" and "*work* the *work* at the tabernacle." Clearly, the Levites were supposed *to guard* and *to work* in the tabernacle.

Likewise, several chapters later, these same two verbs are applied to Aaron and his sons:

> And you and your sons with you shall *guard* your priesthood for all that concerns the altar and that is within the veil; and you shall *serve* [lit. *work*]. I give your priesthood as a gift, and any outsider who comes near shall be put to death. (Num 18:7)

Given the priestly character of this terminology in the context of the whole of Scripture, we see that from the very beginning Adam is being put into the Garden of Eden as the primordial priest.[1] Not only that, but Eden is

---

[1] For a stellar summary of the evidence for Adam-as-priest, see Jeffrey

the primordial sanctuary. In Genesis 2:10–12, the sacred author describes it in this way:

> A river flowed out of Eden to water the [G]arden, and there it divided and became four rivers. The name of the first is Pishon, it is the one that flows around the whole land of Havilah, where there is gold. And the gold of that land is good; bdellium and onyx stone are there.

The Garden of Eden has a river flowing out of it, and nearby—readily available—are gold and precious stones. These materials are very significant. Later in the Book of Exodus, when the tabernacle, a kind of moving temple, was being built under Moses, he received instructions for the vestments of the high priest. Exodus 28:17–20 tells us about the breastplate of the high priest:

> You shall set in it four rows of stones. A row of sardius, topaz, and carbuncle shall be in the first row; and in the second row an emerald, a sapphire, and a diamond; and the third row a jacinth, an agate, and an amethyst; and the fourth row, a ber-

Morrow, "Work as Worship in the Garden and the Workshop: Genesis 1–3, the Feast of St. Joseph the Worker, and Liturgical Hermeneutics," in *Logos: A Journal of Catholic Thought and Culture* 15.4 (2012): 159–178. See also John Bergsma, "The Creation Narratives and the Original Unity of Work and Worship in the Human Vocation," in *Work: Theological Foundations and Practical Implications*, eds. R. Keith Loftin & Trey Dimsdale (London: SCM Press, 2018), 11–29.

yl, an onyx, and a jasper; they shall be set in gold filigree.

This is just one of many examples of how gems and gold were necessary for the construction of the place of worship. So we see that the Garden of Eden is well situated and well provided. It is situated near these precious metals and gemstones, which are necessary to create the beauty that befits the worship of God.

In 1 Chronicles 29:2, we have an account of David describing his preparations for the building of the Temple, which was the successor of the tabernacle. David says,

> So I have provided for the house of my God, so far as I was able, the gold for the things of gold, the silver for the things of silver, and the bronze for the things of bronze, the iron for the things of iron, and wood for the things of wood, besides great quantities of onyx and stones for setting, antimony, colored stones, all sorts of precious stones, and marble.

Notice how onyx is singled out here. Onyx was probably the primary precious gemstone used in the vestments, furnishings, and decorations of the Temple. We can go so far as to identify onyx as a "sacred stone." This is confirmed by the prophet Ezekiel, who sees a vision where a certain character, whom the Church has traditionally identified as Lucifer, is being described. This Lucifer or Lucifer-like character is described by God as having been in Eden:

> You were in Eden, the garden of God; every precious stone was your covering, carnelian, topaz, and jasper, chrysolite, beryl, and onyx, sapphire, carbuncle, and emerald; and wrought in gold were your settings and your engravings. On the day that you were created they were prepared. (Ezek 28:13)

This passage supplements the account of Genesis 2 by describing the Garden of Eden as a place of many precious gemstones and gold. The prophet Ezekiel also has a vision of a future temple:

> Then he brought me back to the door of the temple; and behold, water was issuing from below the threshold of the temple toward the east (for the temple faced east); and the water was flowing down from below the right side of the threshold of the temple, south of the altar. (Ezek 47:1)

Let's place Ezekiel in salvation history. In the days of this prophet, the kingdom of David had long ago gone into decline. Eventually it was captured by the Babylonians, and the people of Judah were carried off to Babylon in 597 BC. Ezekiel is prophesying during this period, speaking to those Judeans who were already in exile. By this time the Temple of Solomon had been destroyed, but the prophet sees a vision of a new temple, and in this vision he sees a river flowing out from the Temple. What's the origin of this river? To where does that concept constantly point back to? Obviously, to *Eden*, this Garden from which flowed a river that watered the whole earth. Eden is the original *type* of the Temple—it's the *primordial temple*.

This brief survey of passages helps us to unlock a key dimension of salvation history. When we look at how the tabernacle built by Moses and how the Temple built by Solomon were decorated, we find in common with both those sanctuaries ample use of gold, gemstones, the presence of cherubim, and the presence of floral and faunal motifs (i.e., animals and plants). Both the tabernacle and the Temple were decorated in such a way as to resemble a garden. Why? What was the point? It is that the tabernacle—and then later the Temple—were places that people could go to experience the presence of God, that presence of God from which Adam was cast out. These sanctuaries provided a way to return to God and "[walk with him] in the cool of the day" (Gen 3:8), in the kind of intimacy and relationship that Adam once enjoyed.

## THE FIRST PRIEST IN THE FIRST SANCTUARY

Putting all this data together, we can see that Adam was the original priest in the original sanctuary. But if Eden is the *sanctuary,* the inner part of the temple often called the "Holy Place," where is the original temple that contained it? Let's look to the account of the days of creation in Genesis 1. The structure of this chapter reveals that the cosmos itself was in some sense a temple, and Eden was, as it were, the navel of the cosmos where the temple nature of the entire universe is concentrated.

One of the clearest indications of this is in Genesis 1:14, which is recounting the fourth day of creation: "And God said, 'Let there be lights in the firmament of the heavens to separate the day from the night; and let them be for signs and for seasons and for days and years.'" The word used for *seasons* does not refer primarily to meteorological or astronomical divisions of time or climate. It's talking about *liturgical seasons.* The Hebrew word is *mo'edim,* and in the Hebrew language to this very day it refers to festivals of the liturgical calendar.

So what was God's purpose in putting the great lights as "signs" up in the sky for the telling of time? It was to regulate the liturgical calendar. Thus, we can see that from the beginning there was a *liturgical purpose* for creation. Creation itself is constructed in the basic unit of liturgical time, the seven-day week culminating with the Sabbath, itself the day of rest and worship.

We find another clue to the liturgical nature of creation at the end of the account of the seven days. In

Genesis 2:1–3 we read,

> Thus the heavens and the earth were finished,
> and all the host of them. And on the seventh day
> God finished his work which he had done, and he
> rested on the seventh day from all his work which
> he had done. So God blessed the seventh day and
> hallowed it, because on it God rested from all his
> work which he had done in creation.

The writing style here is particularly wonderful in the
ancient Hebrew. This probably came from the oral traditions, passed on by listening again and again to these
truths about God, learning by hearing and then passing
on that tradition to one's children. But let's compare this
passage at the end of creation week to the account in Exodus where Moses and the people of Israel finished con-
structing their movable temple—the tabernacle—in the
desert:

> Thus all the work of the tabernacle of the tent of
> meeting was finished; and the sons of Israel had
> done according to all the Lord had commanded
> Moses. . . . And Moses saw all the work, and be-
> hold, they had done it; as the Lord had command-
> ed, so had they done it. And Moses blessed them."
> (Exod 39:32, 43)

As in Genesis, we see that there is a blessing upon finishing the work of temple-building.

These verbal echoes are not accidental at all. The finishing of creation and the finishing of the tabernacle reflect one another, and both passages shed light on one another. Just as the cosmos is a macro-temple, so we can also say the tabernacle (and later, the Temple) is a microcosm or a "small universe."

This is a beautiful image because when we get to the New Testament, to the Gospel of John, Jesus' body is going to become our new temple (John 2:21), and he brings about a new creation (2 Cor 5:17; Rev 21:5). We can see how temple and creation are intertwined: every temple is a microcosm of creation. We see this today in church architecture. A well-built church helps us enter into the worship of the cosmos. For example, a vaulted ceiling of deep blue, with stars, saints, and the angels gives us a real sense when entering into church that we are now in the cosmic temple prepared to worship the Redeemer of the whole universe, our Lord and Savior Jesus Christ.

So this temple–sanctuary–priesthood concept goes back to the very beginning of Scripture. Adam himself had a priestly role in a sanctuary that was the Garden of Eden. And what Adam enjoyed prior to the Fall gives us an idea of what God meant for us, and what has been restored to us in Christ: *priesthood*.

While the roles of Adam's kingship and his prophet-hood can be distinguished from his priesthood, they are never truly separated from it and form a triad of complementary capacities that flow naturally from Adam's sonship. For example, in Genesis 1:26 and 1:28 we read that God gave Adam dominion (Hebrew *radah*) over all the creation, that he should subdue (Hebrew *kavash*) all of it. These are, without doubt, royal terms; indeed, they are imperial terminology, because we find them later used to describe the growth of David's empire (2 Sam 8:11, *kavash*) and the imperial rule of his greater son Solomon (1 Kgs 4:24; 5:16; 9:23). The sacred author portrays Adam as a king or emperor over all creation, and Eden will serve not only as Temple but royal palace. This royal perspective on Adam continues to be reflected in other, later biblical texts, notably Psalm 8:

> What is man [Hebrew *enosh*] that you are mind-
>     ful of him,
> The son of man [Hebrew *ben-'adam*] that you
>     care for him?
> Yet you have made him a little lower than the
>     heavenly beings
> and crowned him with glory and honor.
> You have made him ruler [Hebrew *mashal*] over
>     the works of your hands;
> you have put all things under his feet,

all sheep and oxen,

and also the beasts of the field,

the birds of the heavens, and the fish of the sea,

whatever passes along the paths of the seas. (Ps
8:4–8, my translation)

The Psalmist seems, among other things, consciously to be reflecting on the creation account of Genesis 1, as he re-uses many of the key phrases and concepts, even referring to the human race poetically as the "son of Adam" (Hebrew *ben-adam*).

Then there is Adam's role of prophet, which is subtly presented and commonly missed, but once recognized cannot be "unseen." In Genesis 2:18–20 we have the account of creation and naming of the animals. These verses present us with several novelties. For the first time in the narrative, something is "not good"—Adam's loneliness. Also for the first time, someone other than God gives a name to an aspect of creation. So far, God has given names to the Day and Night (1:5), the Heavens (1:8), the Earth and Seas (1:10), and by implication, other aspects of creation as well. But now for the first time, God creates something—animals—and another person ascribes the name.

Naming was immensely important in the ancient world, and ancient Israel was no exception. The *name* of a person *represented* the person and actualized his or her presence when invoked. The gift of the name sealed the coming-into-existence of a thing and defined its (or his or her) nature. Without a name, a thing was not fully existent. Adam's act of bestowing a name was a participation in God's creative activity, like placing the capstone on a piece of architecture. Moreover, naming cannot be done without speaking—indeed, the act of naming is a kind of speech-act, a way of "doing something with words." This speaking was authoritatively backed by the permission of God. It was final and definitive, as indicated by the sacred author: "[God] brought them to the man to see what he would call them. And whatever the man called every living creature, that was its name" (Gen 2:19). In other words, God allowed Adam to speak with an authority that rightfully belonged to God Himself; as Creator, the right of naming was His.

Someone who speaks authoritatively on behalf of God we call a prophet. Therefore, Adam also exercised a prophetic role. He enjoyed all three of the roles typically associated with being "anointed": prophet, priest, and king. All flow from his divine sonship, which uniquely suited him to represent God in the roles of teaching (prophethood), governing (kingship), and worship (priesthood).

In the ancient world there was no distinction between "Church" and "State." The human community was both a political and religious body. Therefore, the ideal ruler always combined the roles of prophet, priest, and king. In a particular way we see this in the great monarchs of Israel: King David, who spoke by God's Spirit (2 Sam 23:2; Acts 2:29–30) and led the worshiping congregation of Israel in priestly garb (2 Sam 6:12–19; 2 Sam 8:17), and Solomon, through whom spoke the Spirit of divine wisdom (1 Kgs 4:29–34 ET; Wis 7:7) and who functioned as a priest in blessing and sacrifice at the consecration of the Temple (1 Kings 8:14; 54–64). Obviously, Jesus also exercises this triple role.

The integration of these roles is still manifest today in the Catholic Church, a "perfect society" in the philosophical sense, which is actually the kingdom of David, ruled over by those who have succeeded to the princely role of the Apostles (Luke 22:30). In each local church, the bishop teaches as a prophet, governs as a king, and sanctifies as a priest. The laity also share these roles according to their state.[2] Thus, although we intend to trace only the role and theme of priesthood through Scripture, priesthood is not—in the plan of God—separated from other roles for which he destined humanity, such as ruling creation and speaking on his behalf.

But let us return to the text of Genesis and the creation narrative and consider the priestly description of Adam and the other liturgical images we have observed

---

[2] Catechism of the Catholic Church, 2nd ed. (Washington, DC: United States Conference of Catholic Bishops: 2000), § 900–909 (hereafter cited in text as CCC).

in the text. We see in Adam that God created man in the Garden and gave him a priestly role from the beginning. This shows us—with apologies to the scientists among us—that we are not primarily *homo erectus*. The primary attribute of humanity is not that we stand erect. Nor is it what differentiates us from the animals. And it's not even so much that we're *homo sapiens*—thinking man—as if our thought is what primarily separates us from the animals. Rather, we are *homo liturgicus*: we are worshiping man, and this spiritual dimension is the greatest gulf that separates us from the rest of creation. But "separate" is not the best word. God is really calling Adam to take the glory of the inanimate creation and the glory of the irrational animals into ourselves, and on behalf of the stones that cannot speak and the birds and the fish and animals that cannot speak, to offer praise to God on behalf of the whole universe. That is our true role as human beings.

We all have this role to worship. We share in his priesthood when we are baptized into Christ. We'll unpack what it means to share in Christ's priesthood later, but we know it was God's intention from the beginning that we have this worshiping role, this *priestly* role.

## SACRIFICE, BLESSING, AND COVENANT

What are the duties of priesthood? While there are many relevant passages of the Old Testament, there are, at the least, two essential duties: to sacrifice and to bless. Sacrifice was, arguably, the primary act of the priesthood toward God. It was an act of worship. It was an act to call down the grace of God. Blessing, in contrast, was the primary priestly act toward the rest of the creation, especially the people of God. Priests propitiated God by sacrifice and blessed the people on behalf of God. The acts of sacrificing and blessing renewed and extended the covenant relationship between God and his people.

In other words, the role of the priesthood is very closely related to the maintenance of the covenant relationship with God. Covenants were made and reaffirmed by sacrifice. We see this reflected in Psalm 50:5: "Gather to me my faithful ones, the Lord says, who made a covenant with me by sacrifice." Priesthood is a matter of offering sacrifice, and it takes place within a covenantal relationship. Forming a covenant establishes a family relationship with God, and thereafter the acts of the priesthood maintain, reaffirm, and renew that covenant relationship.

Let's go back to Adam. Certainly we can understand how he might *bless* his children and his wife, but what was his *sacrifice*? After all, in Hebrews 8:3 it says, "every high priest is appointed to offer gifts and sacrifices; hence it is necessary for this priest also to have something to offer." Of course, this text is talking about Jesus, but it does establish the basic principle that it's necessary for a priest to have something to offer and to sacrifice. What was Adam supposed to offer in sacrifice?

To answer this question let's return to Genesis 2:15: "The Lord God took the man and put him in the Garden of Eden to till it and to guard it" (my translation). What does it mean for Adam to "guard" Eden? To guard it from what? We have a tendency to think that at creation everything was completely peaceful, but there's another way of looking at it. Some scholars have argued the creation was good—in fact, very good—but that it needed to be tamed. In other words, that's the purpose behind God speaking of the first human beings having "dominion": namely, let them bring greater order and peace to creation.

Some Old Testament scholars argue that God's intention was for the perfect peace of the Garden of Eden to be protected by Adam and then advanced out through the whole world. The "work" Adam was to do was to extend the peace of the Garden throughout the whole creation and extend his dominion over all creation.

In Genesis 3:1 we are confronted immediately by the serpent. Are snakes ever a good thing in the Bible? Surely not. For the ancient Israelites living in the land of Israel, almost all snakes were poisonous. For people living in the wilderness, a snake was a flexible, quick-moving instrument of death. And that's all they knew about snakes: Stay away from them! Snakes are just not a good thing from a Hebrew perspective:

> Now the serpent was more subtle than any other wild creature that the Lord God had made. He said to the woman, "Did God say, 'You shall not eat of any tree of the Garden?'" And the woman said to the serpent, "We may eat of the fruit of the trees of the garden; but God said, 'You shall not eat of the fruit of the tree which is in the midst of the garden, neither shall you touch it, lest you die.'" But the serpent said to the woman, "You will not die. For God knows that when you eat of it your eyes will be opened, and you will be like God, knowing good and evil." (Gen 3:1–5)

Notice that in the midst of their conversation the serpent directly contradicts God, telling Eve, "You will not die" if you eat the fruit.

What's the dynamic here? Is it merely an attempt at deception? Let's speculate that there is something more than just deception. Is it also *intimidation*? A serpent was a threatening creature. The Hebrew word here, *nahash*, can refer to a smaller creature like a snake or worm, but it can also be used for a large dragon. For example, in the Book of Job, *nahash* is used to describe *Rahab*, a primordial serpent creature of great evil (Job 26:12–13). In Egyptian mythology, the great Sun God Amon-Re struggled with Apep the chief demon and chaos-monster (a kind of Egyptian Satan figure), who was embodied as a giant snake. So Genesis 3 may be communicating that this serpent is something much more intimidating than what you might see slithering through your garden. But even if we think of just an ordinary snake, remember that they are all poisonous, potentially lethal creatures from the perspective of the Israelites. So, either way, in addition to deception, there appears to be an element of *intimidation* in the Genesis narrative.

## Adam's Passivity and the End of His Priesthood

But who was put in the Garden to guard it? Eve wasn't told to guard the Garden. Someone else was. It is not clear exactly what Adam is doing at the beginning of Genesis 3, but we're on firm ground in asserting that he is *negligently passive* in the account. For some reason, many English translations do not fully translate verse six, which reads in the Hebrew: "she took of its fruit and ate, and she also gave some to her husband *who was with her.*" That last phrase, often left untranslated, makes it clear that Adam had been there the whole time and yet did nothing. When Eve gave him the fruit, Adam did not protest or recall the commandment of God. He simply took it and ate. He did nothing to confront the serpent.

How does this relate to Adam's sacrifice? I would suggest that Adam's sacrifice was to be his *very self*. God put Adam in the Garden and allowed the serpent to test him, and Adam's role was to oppose that serpent. Despite the fact that the serpent was intimidating and Adam undoubtedly knew he was risking his life to oppose him, Adam had to "guard" the Garden and drive out the serpent to fulfill his priestly role. He was called, I believe, to be willing to do that in obedience to God, even if it meant the possibility of his own death. Adam needed to consent to the potential sacrifice of his own life, his own body, in the act of opposing the serpent for the sake of his bride. Had he done so, God would have assisted him. But instead Adam was negligently passive, even cowardly.

If this interpretation is correct, it offers a deeper insight into a scriptural theme that culminates with Christ laying down his life for his Bride. It also follows the pattern of Adam's "priestly sacrifice" that took place prior to the Fall into sin. In Genesis 1–2, there is only one thing found wrong with all creation, only one thing amiss, only one thing that might be called, in a qualified sense, "evil" inasmuch as it was a privation of good. It was that man was alone: "It is not good that the man should be alone" (Gen 2:18).

How does Adam have to respond to this one "evil" in creation? First, God brings all the animals to him, but not a single animal is fit to give up its natural role, to "sacrifice" its place in the ecosystem, if you will, in order to become man's companion. So God places Adam into a death-like sleep, and cuts his flesh, shedding his blood, in order to remove the rib which he builds into the woman, Eve. Thus, to correct the one privation found in all creation prior to the Fall, it was necessary for Adam to die to self and sacrifice his body. I would suggest this is the paradigm of Adam's priestly role: his sacrificial victim was his own self, his own "body," as St. Paul says in Romans 12:1: "I appeal to you therefore, brethren, by the mercies of God, to present your bodies as a living sacrifice, holy and acceptable to God, which is your spiritual worship." Adam was willing to perform this self-sacrifice the first time so that Eve could come forth; but the second time his faith and courage fail, when Eve is threatened in Genesis 3.

Adam and Eve succumbed to the temptation, and this leads naturally to ask, what happens to the priesthood? Humanity falls into sin and turns away from God, and the relationship with God is damaged. Adam is cast out of his sanctuary and it appears that he's not able to perform his priestly functions. So this priesthood appears to cease. Mankind descends into sin (Genesis 4–6). Eventually, God grieves that he's made mankind because of the violence that fills the earth (Gen 6:5–6).

God decides to send the flood to cleanse the earth and

he will start over with the most righteous man, Noah, who becomes a new Adam figure, a new father, a new "first man" of the human race. Noah builds the ark and takes in plants and animals. The ark is built with three stories or decks (6:16), which, not coincidentally, is how the Temple will later be built (1 Kings 6:6). He floats through the flood. At the end of the flood, the dry land comes up out of the waters (Gen 8:14), just as it did in creation (Gen 1:9). Noah lands on the top of the mountains of Ararat (Gen 8:4), just as Eden was a mountain. When he disembarks from the ark, Genesis 8:20 describes his first act: "Then Noah built an altar to the Lord, and took of every clean animal and of every clean bird, and offered burnt offerings on the altar."

Noah, as a new father of all humanity, resumes here the priestly role of Adam. He offers sacrifice, something that later in Israel's history was limited to the sons of Aaron alone. Noah takes up the priesthood that was lost, as it were, by the Fall into sin. And notice that this priestly offering of sacrifice is related to the *covenant*. In the next chapter, after the sacred author describes God as "smelling the pleasing aroma" of Noah's sacrifice, we read: "Then God said to Noah and his sons with him, 'Behold, I establish my *covenant* with you and your descendants after you'" (Gen 9:8–9).

## ADAM'S PRIESTHOOD RE-ESTABLISHED IN NOAH

Throughout Scripture, sacrifice plays a role in the renewal of covenants. The sacrifice of Noah becomes the occasion of God's "remembering" or renewing the covenant that he had originally formed with Adam.

The Hebrew word used in Genesis 9:8 for the making of the covenant with Noah is *hêqîm*, which we usually translate as "establish." But it is not the typical word used for initiating a covenant with someone in the Bible, which is *karath*, "to cut." One "cut" a covenant because making a covenant initially usually involved cutting animals in sacrifice. But *hêqîm* in Gen 9:8 is, arguably, a word that's more commonly used for *reaffirming, renewing,* or *maintaining* a covenant that is already in existence. Literally, it means, "to make [something] rise or stand up," thus it may convey the sense of "stand something back up that has fallen down," or to renew or to re-establish. This suggests that the covenant that existed between God and Adam is now being renewed between God and Noah, a second father figure.

The ancient Israelites were very attentive to the priestly acts that were performed by Noah and those that followed him. The Hebrew tradition held that the priesthood was, as it were, re-established in Noah after the flood, and then passed down from patriarch to patriarch until the time of Moses. This ancient Hebrew tradition is, in fact, recorded for us in the Catholic *Glossa Ordinaria*, often called by scholars simply "the *Glossa*." The *Glossa* was the standard body of commentary notes that were written in the margins of medieval Bibles, a kind of medieval "study Bible." Commenting on Gen 14:18, the *Glossa* says: "The Hebrews claimed that every patriarch from Noah to Aaron was a priest and that the priesthood was passed from father to son."[3] The writers of the *Glossa* got this from the medieval rabbis, but it is an ancient Israelite way of reading Scripture, and was probably intended by the sacred authors.

Consistently in the Old Testament we see the patriarchs in the role of priests, which reveals to us that fatherhood is a natural priesthood, and conversely, priesthood is a supernatural fatherhood. This relationship between fatherhood and priesthood affects the way we address our priests even to this day.

## PRIESTHOOD OF THE PATRIARCHS

Let's continue to follow the priesthood through salvation history and look at the priesthood of the patriarchs. We begin with the great patriarch Abram, who was called by God in Genesis 12:1–3 and told to move from Ur of the Chaldees (modern-day Kuwait/Iraq) to the Prom-

---

[3] *Glossa Ordinaria*, vol. 1b (The Lollard Society, 1270–1349), https://www.lollardsociety.org/glor/Glossa_vol1b_Genesis.pdf, 204.

ised Land, Canaan (roughly modern Israel). There, God was going to make him a numerous people and grant him great blessings. Through Abram all the families of the earth would be blessed (Gen 12:2–3). That's significant, of course, because blessing others is fundamentally a priestly role.

Abraham obeyed God in faith and moved his family into the land of Canaan. A few verses after God's initial call in Genesis 12, we read: "Thence he removed to the mountain on the east of Bethel, and pitched his tent, with Bethel on the West and Ai on the east; and there he built an altar to the Lord and called on the name of the Lord" (Gen 12:8). This act of "calling upon the name of the Lord" is an ancient liturgical practice. It's an idiomatic phrase meaning that he performed the actions of worship, offering sacrifice and prayer to God. In other words, he was behaving as a priest. Abram continues this priestly activity throughout his life.[4]

Interestingly, the scriptural story of Abraham records a character who apparently exercised a greater priesthood than Abraham's. We see this in Genesis 14. Abraham has accomplished a great military victory, rescuing his nephew Lot and his fellow citizens from some Mesopotamian kings. Then we read:

＊

---

[4] Gen 13:4, 18; 15:9; Gen 21:33; 22:1–19.

After his return from the defeat of Chedorlao-
mer and the kings who were with him, the king
of Sodom went out to meet him at the Valley of
Shaveh (that is, the King's Valley). And Melchizedek king of Salem brought out bread and wine.
(Gen 14:17–18)

In Hebrew, *melech* means "king" and "*zedek*" means righteous, so his name means "righteous king" or "king of righ-
teousness." *Salem* means peace (a form of *shalom*), and it's
the archaic name for the city later called *Jeru-Salem.* One
can also find Jerusalem referred to as "Salem" in Egyptian conquest inscriptions from pre-Israelite times. When
the biblical text says that the "king of Salem" (Jerusalem)
brought out bread and wine, this was not just a post-bat-
tle meal. The sacred author mentions that Melchizedek
was a priest to God Most High for a reason. This was a
liturgical sacrifice, a libation. The wine was for libation
and the bread was for an offering, just as later, in the sacrificial regulations of Moses, we will discover that not all
offerings were sacrificial animals. Grain or baked goods
could constitute on offering as well (Lev 2:1–16). After
the offering, Melchizedek blessed Abram and said:

"Blessed be Abram by God Most High, maker of
heaven and earth; and blessed be God Most High
who has delivered your enemies into your hand!"

and Abram gave him a tenth of everything. (Gen 14:19–20)

Here we have a figure whose priesthood is apparently greater than Abraham, since he blesses Abraham. The author of the Book of Hebrews—perhaps Paul—will make quite a big deal out of the priesthood of Melchizedek. The ancient Jews puzzled over the identity of this mysterious figure. Who was this man superior to Abraham? The consensus was that Melchizedek was Shem, the oldest son of Noah. Their reasoning was this: If you look at the lifespans of the ancient patriarchs, Shem lives into the time of Abraham (Gen 11:10–11). And so, if Shem was still alive in Abraham's day, he must have exercised a greater priesthood than Abraham's, since he is Abraham's forefather. Thus the *Targums*—the ancient translations of Scripture into the common language (Aramaic) of the Jews of Jesus' day—regularly identify Melchizedek as Shem.

Melchizedek is one of the more famous types of Christ in the Old Testament. Like Adam, he combines in one person the roles of *kingship* and *priesthood*. We will come back to Melchizedek later when we treat the Epistle to the Hebrews, but let's return to Abraham and his covenant with God.

## ABRAHAMIC COVENANT

There are three stages to the Abrahamic covenant. The first stage is detailed in Genesis 15, where God instructs Abram to cut several animals in half and lay the pieces opposite one another. After darkness falls, God's presence appears as a flaming torch and burning fire pot (like a thurible) and passes through the pieces of the animals. That was an ancient covenant-making ritual, which established God and Abraham as family members. The blessings associated with this new family relationship were numerous descendants and land (Gen 15:13–20), the ingredients to become a "great nation" (Gen 12:2).

The second stage of the covenant is related in Genesis 17. God again appears to Abraham, after the fiasco with Hagar that resulted in the unintended son Ishmael, and re-makes the covenant with Abraham. Now, God adds an explicit promise that kingship will come from Abraham, and he institutes circumcision as the sign of the covenant, a ritual that in one sense can be interpreted as a symbolic rebuke of Abraham's powers of procreation that had been misused in the previous chapter (Gen 16).

Finally, in Genesis 22 we come to the great covenant test. To understand the significance of this test it's important to grasp that a covenant is centered around a relationship—that it is not merely a contractual agreement. A covenant makes you family. Modern forms of covenant would be marriage or adoption, legal arrangements that make you family.

Family members need to be loyal to one another. They need to trust one another. In Hebrew, the term for this love that family members and covenant partners have for one another is *hesed*; it is translated in the Psalms as "steadfast love," although the ancient translations rendered it "mercy." We are all familiar with Lamentations 3:22: "The steadfast love [*hesed*] of the Lord never ceases, his mercies [*raham*] never come to an end." These are two covenant terms that affirm the kind of indissoluble, unchanging commitment covenant partners have toward one another: faithful love [*hesed*] and compassion [*raham*].

In Genesis 22, God is going to test Abraham's covenant faithfulness, his *hesed*. He asks Abraham to do a priestly act, but it's a priestly act of a rather severe nature:

> After these things God tested Abraham, and said to him, "Abraham!" And he said, "Here am I." He said, "Take your son, your only son Isaac, whom you love, and go to the land of Mori'ah, and offer him there as a burnt offering upon one of the mountains of which I shall tell you." (Gen 22:1–2)

There are two things to notice immediately. First, the phrase "your only son Isaac" can also be translated "your *only-begotten* son Isaac." This picks up the connection with John 3:16. Many scholars believe that the Hebrew word *yahid*, "one and only, unique," which is used three times in Genesis 22 to describe Isaac, is translated as *monogenēs* in the Greek of John 3:16, coming out in English as "only-begotten." Second, God commands Abraham to perform the priestly act of offering a sacrifice at a sacred place (a mountain). The mountain is in the land of Moriah, which Jewish tradition identified as the precise peak on which Solomon built the Temple years later (2 Chr 3:1).

Abraham and Isaac traveled together to this mountain in the land of Moriah, and they began to walk up the mountain: "And Abraham took the wood of the burnt offering, and laid it on Isaac his son; and he took in his hand the fire and the knife. So they went both of them together" (Gen 22:6). Notice that Isaac is made to carry the wood. You need a lot of wood to burn up a sacrifice, so the load of wood is a heavy burden. Isaac is made to carry it, which tells us that Isaac, by this time in the narrative, was a strapping young man. In fact, he's called by the same term—*na'ar*—used to describe the "young men" (*na'arîm*) who accompany Abraham on this journey as servants and bodyguards (Gen 22:5). Isaac is not the five-year-old we sometimes see pictured in illustrated children's Bibles. He's a young man, stronger than his father Abraham, who is, in fact, over one hundred years old by this time.

As they are walking up the mountain together, Isaac asks his father about the animal of sacrifice: "[Isaac] said, 'Behold, the fire and the wood; but where is the lamb for a burnt offering?' Abraham said, 'God will provide himself the lamb for a burnt offering, my son'" (Gen 22:7–8). Abraham's response is one of the most beautiful verses of the Old Testament. The RSVCE translates the Hebrew phrase very well, since it can be taken in different ways. First, that the Lord himself will go out and find a lamb for the burnt offering. Second, that the Lord will provide himself *as* the lamb for the burnt offering.[5] One meaning is fulfilled almost immediately in Genesis 22, as the ram is caught in the thicket; while the second meaning is fulfilled in John 19, the crucifixion.

When they reach the top of the mountain, Abraham proceeds to perform the actions necessary to sacrifice Isaac. Because Isaac was stronger than his aged father, he obviously could have overpowered Abraham or run away. In other words, this was not something that Isaac was *compelled* to do. In the Jewish tradition, the rabbis understood from ancient times that Isaac freely accepted his place as

---

[5] The Hebrew reads, very literally: "God will see to himself a lamb for the burnt offering, my son." Hebrew "see" can mean "provide," so this could be taken as: "God will provide for himself a lamb for the burnt offering." But also, "God will look to himself: a lamb for the burnt offering!" The LXX translates: "God will perceive in himself the lamb for the burnt offering, child."

victim of sacrifice.[6]

Isaac is the only-begotten son carrying the wood of his sacrifice up the mountain to offer himself to God. Although the typology is quite clear, more importantly, for present purposes, we see in Genesis 22 *a priestly act being performed*. There is cooperation between the father and son. The father is priest, but the son is also priest and victim, freely handing himself over for the sacrifice.

Without understanding Isaac's age, maturity, and consent, Genesis 22 can seem like a terrible moral dilemma. How could God ask for human sacrifice, especially for a father to sacrifice his own son? But human sacrifice is not the point at issue in this narrative. Rather, it's a test of the faith of Abraham and Isaac. Seen in light of the cross of Jesus, which this event foreshadows, we can see that God is testing Abraham and Isaac, asking them to demonstrate their willingness to enter into the suffering love of the Trinity; indeed, their willingness to participate in the very kind of sacrifice that the Holy Trinity will need to perform to save all mankind. And Abraham and Isaac pass that test!

In response to their faith, God makes this promise

---

[6] In the ancient Targum Neofiti, Isaac insists that Abraham bind him tight so that he doesn't flinch at the moment of sacrifice. In Targum Pseudo-Jonathan, the Lord's command to Abraham to sacrifice Isaac is provoked by Isaac's boast to Ishmael that he (Isaac) would never refuse God the sacrifice of any part of his body.

to Abraham: "By myself I have sworn, says the Lord, because you have done this, and have not withheld your son, your only son, I will indeed bless you, and I will multiply your descendants as the stars of heaven and as the sand which is on the seashore. And your descendants shall possess the gate of their enemies, and by your descendants [literally, by your seed] shall all the nations of the earth bless themselves, because you have obeyed my voice" (Gen 22:16–18). The promise of blessing through the seed of Abraham is a messianic promise.

The sacrifice embraced by Abraham and Isaac would be carried out in earnest thousands of years later at nearly the same site, because later the temple was built where Abraham offered Isaac, and Calvary was but a stone's throw from the Temple. This later sacrifice would result in the death of the only-begotten Son of God the Father. In fulfillment of the role of Isaac, Jesus is both priest and victim, making Genesis 22 the "Calvary of the Old Testament," the great foundational event for the rest of salvation history. It also illustrates the relationship between *fatherhood* and *priesthood, sacrifice,* and *covenant.* The *father* is a *priest* who offers the *sacrifice* that renews the *covenant.*

## SUMMARY

In this chapter we demonstrated how the idea of the

priesthood goes back to the very beginnings of Scripture, implicit in Adam's priestly role in the Garden of Eden: "The Lord God took the man and put him in the Garden of Eden to till it and to keep it" (Gen 2:15). We argued that the literal translation of the Hebrew "till" and "keep" is "work" and "guard," and that these terms in Scripture are closely related to God's priests and sanctuaries, that this terminology in the context of the whole of Scripture strongly indicate that from the very beginning Adam was put into the Garden of Eden as the primordial priest, and Eden was the primordial sanctuary (Gen 2:10–12; Exod 28:17–20; 1 Chr 29:2; Ezek 28:13, 47:1).[7]

We also asserted that the original temple that contained the sanctuary in Eden was the cosmos itself: "And God said, 'Let there be lights in the firmament of the heavens to separate the day from the night; and let them be for signs and for seasons and for days and years'" (Gen 1:14). We noted that the Hebrew word used for *seasons* refers to *liturgical seasons*, and we saw that from the beginning there was a liturgical purpose for creation. Because of this, we argued that a more apt description of humans than *homo erectus* and *homo sapiens* would be *homo litur-*

---

[7]  For more on Eden as the original sanctuary, see my essay, "The Creation Narratives and the Original Unity of Work and Worship in the Human Vocation," in *Work: Theological Foundations and Practical Implications*, eds. R. Keith Loftin & Trey Dimsdale, (London: SCM Press, 2018), 11–29, and the literature I cite therein.

*gicus*—worshiping man, and that we all have this priestly role to worship.

We went on to point out that two essential duties of the priesthood were to sacrifice (Ps 50:5; Heb 8:3) and to bless (Exod 39:32, 43). We showed how sacrifice (an act of worship) was the primary priestly act toward God and how blessing (calling down the grace of God) was the primary priestly act toward the rest of the creation, especially God's people. We further illustrated how acts of sacrifice and blessing renewed and extended the covenant relationship between God and his people, and that the role of the ministerial priesthood was closely related to the maintenance of the covenant.

We looked at how Adam exercised these two priestly duties of sacrifice and blessing, and we noted that while it would have been natural for Adam to *bless* his children and his wife, it would have been much more difficult to sacrifice himself when confronted by the serpent (Gen 3:1). We speculated that in "guarding" the Garden, Adam had to drive out the serpent to fulfill his priestly role, even if his priestly sacrifice could be his very life. We suggested that there appears to be an element of intimidation in the Genesis narrative, that Adam (not Eve) was to guard the Garden, and that he was negligently passive as events unfolded. Adam did not protest or recall the commandment of God. He did nothing to confront the serpent. He timidly took the forbidden fruit from Eve and ate. He failed, was cast out of his sanctuary, and could no longer perform his priestly duties.

We then looked at how God re-established Adam's priesthood in Noah, how sacrifice played a role in the renewal of covenants, how Noah's sacrifice (Gen 8:20) became the occasion of renewing the covenant (Gen 9:8) that God had originally formed with Adam. Continuing this priestly tradition, Abraham acted as a priest and was prepared to offer his son Isaac as a sacrifice, and this priesthood was passed down from patriarch to patriarch until the time of Moses.

## SUGGESTIONS FOR FURTHER READING

Beale, Gregory. "The Temple and the Church's Mission: A Biblical Theology of the Dwelling Place of God." In *New Studies in Biblical Theology 15*. Downers Grove: InterVarsity, 2004.

Smith, Steven C. *The House of the Lord: A Catholic Biblical Theology of God's Temple Presence in the Old and New Testaments*. Steubenville, OH: Franciscan University Press, 2017.

## QUESTIONS

1. Where is the idea of the priesthood first intro-

duced in Scripture? Is an explicit or implicit example of the priesthood given?

2. Where in the Old Testament are the words "to work and to guard" used together? What is the significance of these terms?

3. How were both the tabernacle built by Moses and the temple built by Solomon decorated? What did they represent?

4. What do the "seasons" in Genesis 1:14 refer to?

5. In ancient Israel, what does a name represent?

6. In what ways was Adam a priest, prophet, and king?

7. What are the duties of the priesthood?

8. What role does sacrifice play in the renewal of the covenants?

9. What are the three stages of the Abrahamic covenant?

10. Define the meaning of the term "*hesed*."

# CHAPTER 2

# THE PRIESTHOOD FROM ISAAC TO THE EXILE

## PRIESTHOOD IN THE REST OF GENESIS

In looking at the priesthood of Adam, Noah, and Abraham, we have observed the natural relationship between fatherhood and priesthood. This priesthood continues with Isaac as he takes the place of his father as leader of the tribe. In Genesis 26:25, after the Lord appears to him, Isaac builds an altar and "[calls on] the name of the Lord." As we saw earlier, to "call upon the name of the Lord" is a Hebrew idiom for performing an act of worship, which would include offering sacrifice on the altar he built (why else does one build an altar, after all?). In Genesis 26:27–29 and 28:1–4 we see Isaac blessing his son Jacob, transferring to the next generation the blessing he had received from his father Abraham (Gen 22:15–18). So Isaac carries out both main roles of priesthood: sacrifice and blessing.

Jacob carries on in the footsteps of his father, building altars (Gen 35:6), setting up sacred pillars, pouring out drink offerings and oil (Gen 35:14–15). Likewise, we find Jacob blessing his twelve sons (Gen 48:9–16; 49:1–28).

Joseph, the favorite son of Jacob, has a very important position in the narrative of Genesis, but it is easy to overlook his unique *priestly* role. We are, of course, all familiar with the story arc of Joseph, because doubtless we've watched Dreamworks' *Prince of Egypt*. Some of us may even have read Genesis 37–50! Joseph is the famous favorite son with the "coat of many colors" that provokes his brothers' jealousy, as the interpreter of dreams gifted with prophetic insight, and as a statesmen of high order whose God-given wisdom enables him to navigate the world's then-largest nation through an otherwise-catastrophic seven-year famine.

These are the well-known basics, but Joseph's *priestly* role only becomes apparent upon a closer reading of some of the texts, for example, Genesis 45. In the climactic scene of the narrative, after Joseph has revealed his true identity to his brothers, he says: "So it was not you who sent me here, but God; and he has made me a father to Pharaoh, and lord of all his house and ruler over all the land of Egypt" (Gen 45:8).

What does it mean that Joseph was "a father to Pharaoh"? This is neither the same role as being "lord of all his house" (which meant he was Pharaoh's steward) nor being "ruler over all of Egypt" (which meant he was Pharaoh's prime minister). But personally being a "father" to Pharaoh meant that he was a *priest*, one who consulted God on behalf of Pharaoh, offered prayers and sacrifices for him, and mediated God's blessing to him. This was one of the reasons why he was given the daughter of an Egyptian priest as his wife (Gen 41:45). Pharaoh saw Joseph as a good candidate for a priestly role because he was filled with the spirit of God (Gen 41:38–39), revealed in his ability to interpret the meaning of dreams. Since Joseph is the last great figure of the Book of Genesis, this creates a narrative arc through the Bible's first book in which we move from one priestly figure—Adam, father of all mankind—to another, Joseph, whose wisdom enables him to save all mankind, all Adam's descendants. The chain of descent from Adam to Joseph passed through numerous figures who themselves exercised a priestly role on behalf of their families and, indeed, on behalf of all humanity: Noah, Shem-Melchizedek, Abraham, Isaac, Jacob.

## PRIESTHOOD IN EXODUS

We see in the Book of Exodus the continued development of the role of priest. Strikingly, in Exodus 4:22, when God commissions Moses to go to Pharaoh, God speaks of Israel as "my firstborn son." One cannot read that statement without calling to mind God's original "firstborn son," Adam himself. Genesis began with God's firstborn Adam leaving paradise and losing his priesthood. Exodus begins with God's firstborn Israel leaving an Egyptian hell and regaining his priesthood. When God declares Israel as "firstborn son" in Exodus 4:22, the dignities of Adam are being conferred on Israel as a people.

This point is lost on many readers because Adam's status as firstborn is implicit in the early chapters of Genesis, rather than stated outright. Nonetheless, the exegetical logic is clear and straightforward. In Genesis 1:26, 28, we find that God creates Adam in God's own "image" and "likeness." Much ink has been spilled through human history arguing over to what the "image" and "likeness" of God refers. Genesis provides us with a hermeneutical key explaining what it means to be in the image and likeness of another. In Genesis 5:3 we read that Adam had a *son*, Seth; and this son was in his *image* and *likeness*. This language describes how a *son* is like a *father*. In other words, "image" and "likeness" are the language of sonship, of divine filiation.[1] From the moment that God breathed into Adam's nostrils the "breath of life," which the Fathers identified with the Holy Spirit, Adam became a son in the image and likeness of God his Father, a partaker in the di-

---

[1] See Catherine L. McDowell, *The Image of God in the Garden of Eden*, in Siphrut 15 (Winona Lake: Eisenbrauns, 2015), 131.

vine nature. There is a natural *priesthood* that accompanies being a firstborn son, because the eldest son is the natural representative of the father, and when the father happens to be divine, that representative role constitutes a form of priesthood.

Applying that knowledge to our reading of Exodus, when God declares Israel to be the "firstborn son," he confers a priestly status upon the nation as a whole: Israel is a new Adam. If we misunderstand this, it's very easy to misread the text of Exodus in the framework of liberation theology or Marxist ideology, in materialist and economic terms. But this is not how the text of the Bible itself presents the Exodus. The Israelites are a priestly people, and the primary reason for them to leave Egypt is *for worship*.

We all know Moses' famous cry, "Let my people go!" immortalized in Gospel spirituals, political speeches, and other cultural forms. But Moses' original proclamation on behalf of God was: "Let my people go, that they may *serve* me" (Exod 8:1; emphasis mine), and this is the language of priesthood.

The Hebrew word translated as "serve" is the same word used to speak of Adam's priestly role in the Garden. It is the Hebrew *'abad*, which we translated earlier as "work," and together with *shamar* sums up the priestly role. In contexts related to God, *'abad* refers specifically to *worship*. Thus, the purpose of the Exodus was to get the people out of Egypt so that they could freely worship God in their own place. If they tried to worship God in the land of Egypt, they would be stoned by the Egyptians, because the kind of worship that the true God asked for was offensive to the Egyptians (Exod 8:26). The Promised Land provided a place of safety where they could worship and fulfill their priestly obligations as a priestly people. Theologically, it was a "return to Eden."

We find further confirmation of Israel's priestly role later in Exodus, when Moses leads the people to the foot of Sinai. There, as the people prepare for the revelation of God, the gift of the Law, and the establishment of the covenant on the mountain, Moses declares to them on behalf of God:

> Now therefore, if you will obey my voice and keep my covenant, you shall be my own possession among all peoples; for all the earth is mine, and you shall be to me *a kingship of priests* and a holy nation." (Exod 19:5–6, my translation)

The phrase we have translated "kingship of priests" is the Hebrew *mamleket kohanim*, and it is difficult to render because it has multiple senses. A "kingship of priests" could be a community of kings who are also priests, and therefore a *royal priesthood*. Or, "kingship" could be a synonym for "kingdom," a realm governed by a king, and therefore a *kingdom of priests*.[2] Both senses are true, and we find the New Testament translating this phrase in both ways. St. Peter, in his first letter, quotes this passage from the Greek translation (the Septuagint or LXX) when he calls the Church a "royal priesthood" (1 Pet 2:9). John in Revelation 1:6 and 5:10 seems to follow the rendering "kingdom of priests." Regardless, the point here is that *kingship* and *priesthood* are connected, as we saw from the beginning in Adam who was given royal "dominion" over the whole earth (Gen 1:26, 28)[3] and a priestly role to "work and guard" (Gen 2:15)—king and priest. Exodus 19:5–6 confirms that Israel is the new "firstborn son," and therefore both priest and king.

In Genesis 12:2, God had promised to make Abram into a *great nation*, and here at Sinai God fulfills that by making Abraham's descendants into the greatest kind of nation possible, a nation of priest-kings. Likewise, in Genesis 22:18, God had promised Abraham that his seed would bring *blessing* to all the earth. Israel is the seed of Abraham, and through the Exodus God is making them

---

[2] Exodus 19:6 LXX has *basileion hierateuma*, "royal priesthood," for *mamleḵeṯ kōhănîm*. First Peter 2:9 follows this tradition. For a modern defense of this translational option, see John A. Davies, *A Royal Priesthood: Literary and Intertextual Perspectives on an Image of Israel in Exodus 19:6* (JSOTSS 395; London/New York: T&T Clark, 2004), esp. 61–102.

[3] For example, the word for "exercising dominion" (Heb. *rādah*) in Genesis 1:26, 28 will later be used to describe Solomon's imperial domination of the Near East (1 Kgs 4:24 RSV [Hebrew 5:4]).

into a priestly nation so that they can bless the other nations.

At this point in Exodus, the people as a whole had a priestly status, and the firstborn sons served in a capacity that we would understand as the *ministerial priesthood*, that is, taking practical responsibility for leading the liturgy. So we see two levels of priesthood: a general priesthood of all the people and the ministerial priestly role of those who would lead the worship and sacrifice offered to God. We see this reflected in Exodus 24:4–5:

> And Moses wrote all the words of the Lord. And he rose early in the morning, and built an altar at the foot of the mountain, and twelve pillars, according to the twelve tribes of Israel. And he sent young men of the sons of Israel, who offered burnt offerings and sacrificed peace offerings of oxen to the Lord.

This passage has puzzled readers since antiquity, since it describes "young men" who are clearly performing a priestly act, and yet elsewhere in the Old Testament the priesthood is limited to the tribe of Levi and then even further to the sons of Aaron. But this Levitical-Aaronic priesthood is not established until several chapters later!

How did the Jews in antiquity understand this? Looking at the rabbinic tradition, we see that the rabbis understood these "young men" to be firstborn sons. The oldest Jewish Targum (common-language translation of Scripture) reads in Exodus 24:5 "He sent the *firstborn* of the children of Israel, and they offered up burnt offerings . . ."[4] This is not explicit in the text, but the rabbis recalled the Passover account, when the blood of the lamb saved the firstborn sons of the Israelites from death. After the Passover, in Exodus 13:2, God instructs the Israelites to "consecrate to me all the first-born; whatever is the first to open the womb among the people of Israel, both of man and of beast, is mine." That term "consecrate" is key, because throughout the text of the Old Testament the vast majority of instances that speak of the "consecration" of a male human being are actually in the context of *priestly ordination.*[5]

Sadly, a significant change occurs to this original *priesthood of the firstborn* with the episode of the infamous molten calf in Exodus 32:

> When the people saw that Moses delayed to come down from the mountain, the people gathered themselves together to Aaron, and said to him, "Up, make us gods, who shall go before us; as for this Moses, the man who brought us up out of the land of Egypt, we do not know what has become

---

[4] Chaim Miller, ed., *Chumash, The Gutnick Edition, The Book of Exodus* (United States: Kol Menachem, 2005), 24:5.

[5] For example, Exod 28:3, 41; 29:1, 33, 44; 30:30; 40:13, etc.

of him." And Aaron said to them, "Take off the rings of gold which are in the ears of your wives, your sons, and your daughters, and bring them to me." So all the people took off the rings of gold which were in their ears, and brought them to Aaron. And he received the gold at their hand, and fashioned it with a graving tool, and made a molten calf; and they said, "These are your gods, O Israel, who brought you up out of the land of Egypt!" When Aaron saw this, he built an altar before it; and Aaron made proclamation and said, "Tomorrow shall be a feast to the Lord." And they rose up early on the morrow, and offered burnt offerings and brought peace offerings; and the people sat down to eat and drink, and rose up to play. (Exod 32:1–6)

While this is happening, Moses is on Mount Sinai speaking with the Lord, and he comes down to find the Israelites worshiping the golden calf:

And when Moses saw that the people had broken loose (for Aaron had let them break loose, to their shame among their enemies), then Moses stood in the gate of the camp, and said, "Who is on the Lord's side? Come to me." And all the sons of Levi gathered themselves together to him. And he said to them, "Thus says the Lord God of Israel, 'Put every man his sword on his side, and go back and forth from gate to gate throughout the camp, and slay every man his brother, and every man his companion, and every man his neighbor.'" And the sons of Levi did according to the word of Moses; and there fell of the people that day about three thousand men. And Moses said, "Today you have *ordained* yourselves for the service of the Lord, each one at the cost of his son and of his brother, that he may bestow a blessing upon you this day. (Exod 32:25–29, emphasis mine)

## PRIESTHOOD TRANSFERRED FROM THE FIRSTBORN SONS TO THE TRIBE OF LEVI

This is a turning point in the history of the people of Israel when the priesthood is transferred from the firstborn sons to the tribe of Levi. Now the Levites are responsible for the sanctuary and for the liturgy. This is further confirmed in the Book of Numbers where God instructs Moses to tally up the total of all the firstborn sons and the total of all the Levites, and then make a redemption payment for the discrepancy between these totals (Num 3:40–51). God states the principle clearly: "I have taken the Levites . . . instead of every first-born" (Num 3:12–13).

Notice that the ministerial priestly status of the firstborn of Israel is being taken away from them, that they are being laicized and hereafter the ministerial priesthood will be fulfilled by the tribe of Levi under the direction of the sons of Aaron.

This is a very sad day in the history of Israel. The other eleven tribes can no longer have their firstborn sons serve at the tabernacle. In fact, when God gives instructions for the layout of the camp in the wilderness, the Levites settle around the tabernacle, and the other tribes are situated farther away. The physical distance mirrors the spiritual distance from God's presence. Now, if the other tribes want to come into God's presence, they must go through the Levites. There's an increased distance between the tribes of Israel and God. Whether their common priestly status is totally lost or only damaged is a debatable point, but it is definitely clear that the other tribes have lost the fullness of sonship—including both royalty and priesthood—that they had prior to the worship of the molten calf.

Going forward, the Levites serve in the priestly role, with the descendants of Aaron serving in the role of high priest. They mediate God's presence to the other tribes. One critical dimension of this role was the forgiveness of sin. The priests facilitated the forgiveness of sin, which permitted one to stay in the covenant relationship with God. When someone offended against the covenant, they either came under divine judgment or had to make atonement and receive forgiveness of sins. The Book of Leviticus outlines the process of receiving forgiveness, especially Leviticus 5. For example, we read:

> When a man is guilty in any of these, he shall confess the sin he has committed, and he shall bring his guilt offering to the Lord for the sin which he has committed, a female from the flock, a lamb or a goat, for a sin offering; and the priest shall make atonement for him for his sin. (Lev 5:5–6)

Notice that the guilty party must make a confession of the sin, and the priest had to offer sacrifice on his behalf. In ancient Israel, one could not go to the *prophet* to receive forgiveness, or seek out the *king* to receive absolution. This power resided in the *priest*.

## PRIESTHOOD OF DAVID

The Levitical model of the priesthood continued from the time of Moses until the time of David. During this period of time that extends through the leadership of Joshua, the period of the twelve judges, and the reign of Saul, the Levites fulfill the ministerial priestly role. The other tribes do not seem to be participating actively in the priestly status that they had been offered prior to the sin of worshiping the molten calf (Exod 19:5–6).

But then something strange happens. Beginning in 1 Samuel 16, we encounter an Israelite who is not a Levite and seems to defy some of these categories—King David. When the sacred author first introduces him, we are told that David is the son of Jesse of the tribe of Judah. The prophet Samuel interviews all of Jesse's sons as candidates for the kingship, but God chooses the youngest. When Samuel anoints him with oil, the Spirit of God "[rushes on] David from that day forward." This is what we call the stable possession of the Holy Spirit, something no one had experienced since Adam lost the gift of the Spirit through sin. This presence of the Spirit in David marks him as a new Adam, just as Adam had the "spirit of God" breathed into his nostrils. The infilling of the Holy Spirit helps to explain why we observe David doing many unusual things that suggest a priestly status.

In 1 Samuel 21:1–6, David flees from Saul and takes temporary refuge in the priestly town of Nob, where the Levites and sons of Aaron had set up the tabernacle. There, Ahimelech the high priest feeds David and his men with the bread of the Presence—a type of the Eucharist which only the priests were permitted to eat. Ahimelech grants David a kind of indult in order to eat the bread of the Presence, but the act of eating seems to foreshadow the priestly role that David will exercise during his kingship.

Another good example of this priestly role can be

found in 2 Samuel 6, when David brings the ark of the covenant up into Jerusalem. After replacing Saul as king and gaining the allegiance of all twelve tribes (2 Sam 1–5), David makes Jerusalem, a centrally-located city on the border between the southern and northern tribes, the capital of the kingdom. In David's desire to unify the tribes and focus the national life on worship, he brings the ark to the capital city. This is one of the reasons why David is called a man after God's own heart. He understood the liturgical focus of salvation history—that we are created for worship—and he harnessed his political influence to enhance and prioritize the role of worship in the life of God's people.

The first time David attempted to bring up the ark, they violated canon law by transporting it on an ox cart rather than carrying it on poles, according to its design. As a result, the effort was unsuccessful. Nonetheless, after a brief hiatus, David made another attempt, and this time he was more circumspect to obey God's law. The Levites carried the ark, and every six steps they offered a sacrifice of seven bulls and seven rams. But then the sacred author describes something unusual: David, of the tribe of Judah, is dressed in a robe of fine linen called an *ephod*. This was specifically a priestly garment, like a chasuble would be to us.

And they brought in the ark of God, and set it inside the tent which David had pitched for it; and they offered burnt offerings and peace offerings before God. And when David had finished offering the burnt offerings and the peace offerings, he blessed the people in the name of the Lord" (1 Chr 16:1–2; cf. 2 Sam 6:13–19).

The text describes David as officiating at the altar and offering the sacrifice. Then, he fulfills the second role of the priest by blessing the people "in the name of the Lord." This is particularly striking since in later Jewish tradition, only the high priest was allowed to bless the people in the name of the Lord, typically once a year on the Day of Atonement. But here at the beginning of his reign, David is doing something that later is restricted to the high priest, blessing people with the divine name, which probably means the formula of Numbers 6:24–27.

David then distributes "a loaf of bread, a portion of meat, and a cake of raisins" (2 Sam 6:19; 1 Chr 16:3). There is some debate among scholars regarding the Hebrew word translated as "portion [of meat]." An alternative translation is "a portion of wine," which is very suggestive, since then David would come out offering *bread and wine,* an offering reminiscent of Melchizedek, who (not coincidentally) was the also king of (Jeru)Salem (Gen 14:18).

Another passage of Scripture makes an explicit link between Melchizedek and David. Psalm 110 is called "a psalm of David," which can mean "a psalm written by David," but in this case appears to be "a psalm about David." The voice of the Psalm seems to be the court singer, singing to the king the following:

> The Lord says to my lord:
>> "Sit at my right hand,
>> till I make your enemies your footstool."
> The Lord sends forth from Zion
>> your mighty scepter.
>> Rule in the midst of your foes!
>> Yours is dominion
>> on the day you lead your host
>> in holy splendor.
>> From the womb of the morning
>> I begot you.
> The Lord has sworn
>> and will not change his mind,
>> "You are a priest for ever
>> according to order of Melchizedek." (Ps
>> 110:1–4)

This psalm was understood as a divine oracle that proclaimed a *priestly status* for the Davidic king—not only for David but for his sons in succession. Some scholars think this Psalm functioned as a coronation hymn, along with others like Psalm 2. It was an appropriate piece to be performed for each new son of David as he ascended the throne for the first time.

We can see that David's priesthood was passed on to his heirs in a passage from 2 Samuel, which tells us that "David's sons were priests" (2 Sam 8:18). Many English translations simply have "officials" or another synonym here, but the Hebrew is very clear: *kohanim*, the word for "priests."

But how can David's sons be priests if they aren't Levites? Psalm 110 supplies the answer: the priesthood of David and his descendants comes from Melchizedek. Apparently, the kingship of Jerusalem carried with it a hereditary priesthood. The Israelites considered this priesthood valid since it came down directly from Shem, the son of Noah, who the tradition identified as one and the same with Melchizedek.

The logic of the Bible seems to be that when David conquered Jerusalem—which, for the intervening generations, had been in the hands of the Canaanites—he inherited the priestly office of Melchizedek along with his kingship. In any event, it's clear that he functioned as a priest during the period of his reign over all Israel.

Many of the themes we have highlighted up to this point are brought together in Psalm 89:

> I have found David, my servant;
>> with my holy oil I have anointed him;

so that my hand shall ever abide with him,

my arm also shall strengthen him.

The enemy shall not outwit him,

the wicked shall not humble him.

I will crush his foes before him

and strike down those who hate him.

My faithfulness and my mercy shall be with him,

and in my name shall his horn be exalted.

I will set his hand on the sea

and his right hand on the rivers.

He shall cry to me, "You are my Father,

my God, and the Rock of my salvation."

And I will make him the first-born,

the highest of the kings of the earth.

(Ps 89:20–27)

In the Psalm, David is presented as a new Adam. He is the "first-born": in him, God is re-establishing the unity of the kingly and priestly roles that he had given to Adam in the beginning. Ultimately, he anticipates the second Adam—the "New Adam" in the fullest sense—who is Jesus. But here, in David, we see reintegrated the dignities of Adam and the firstborn sons, lost as a consequence of the sinful worship of the molten calf. Recall that the priesthood of the Levites was not original but that their priesthood was conferred as a consequence of sin.

At this point in the Old Testament, we have two

types of priesthood: the priesthood of the Levites and the priesthood of Melchizedek. After David, the next advance in the development of the priesthood come to us from the great literary prophets who speak of the coming of the Messianic age.

## Priesthood in Isaiah

Isaiah is arguably the greatest of the prophets. The second part of his book (40–66), was understood from ancient times as being one long description of the coming era, often called "the eschatological age" among scholars. "Eschatological" is derived from the Greek *eschatos*, meaning "last" or "final." In Isaiah 56 we see a very important passage for our purposes, which is worth quoting at length:

> Thus says the Lord:
>> Let not the foreigner who has joined himself
>> to the Lord say,
>>> "The Lord will surely separate me from his
>>> people";
>> and let not the eunuch say,
>>> "Behold, I am a dry tree."
>> For thus says the Lord:
>> "To the eunuchs who keep my sabbaths,
>> who choose the things that please me
>> and hold fast my covenant,

I will give in my house and within my walls

a monument and a name

better than sons and daughters;

I will give them an everlasting name

which shall not be cut off.

And the foreigners who join themselves to the
Lord,

to minister to him, to love the name of the
Lord,

and to be his servants,

everyone who keeps the sabbath, and does not
profane it,

and holds fast my covenant—

these I will bring to my holy mountain,

and make them joyful in my house of prayer;

their burnt offerings and their sacrifices

will be accepted on my altar;

for my house shall be called a house of prayer

for all peoples." (Isa 56:1, 3–7)

According to the Law of Moses, eunuchs were not able to participate in the temple worship (Deut 23:2). Foreigners, too, were cut off from the inner precincts of the Temple (Ezek 44:7–9). Although there was an outer court of where Gentiles could come and pray, a wall of separation kept them from the inner parts of the Temple.[6] Yet Isaiah 56 speaks of foreigners "ministering" to the Lord using the Hebrew word *Sharath*, which usually refers to priestly service. It's significant here that we have *priestly language* being used about *foreigners* within Isaiah 40–66, with the implication that they too would minister to the Lord in the Temple in the coming age.

In order for eunuchs and Gentiles to "minister" to the Lord, enter into his house, and offer acceptable sacrifices in the coming age—the era marked by the arrival of the Messiah, whom Isaiah usually calls "the servant of the Lord"—certain aspects of the Mosaic law are going to have to be revoked or at least partially abrogated.[7]

We see a similar teaching in Isaiah 66, in an oracle which is nearly the last in this entire prophetic book:

> For I know their works and their thoughts, and the time is coming to gather all nations and tongues. And they shall come and shall see my glory, and I

---

[6] St. Paul references this in the Letter to the Ephesians, when he writes, "For [Jesus] is our peace, who has made us both one, and has broken down the dividing wall of hostility" (Eph 2:14). It is only with Christ that the division between Jews and Gentiles is overcome. In a certain way, this is prefigured when Jesus cleanses the Temple. The merchants in the Temple were operating in the court of the Gentiles and making it impossible for any Gentile to be recollected in prayer. Jesus specifically references this: "And he taught, and said to them, 'Is it not written, "My house shall be called a house of prayer for all the nations"?' But you have made it a den of robbers" (Mark 11:17).

[7] Exod 12:43–48; Lev 22:25; Deut 23:1–8; Ezek 44:7–9.

will set a sign among them. And from them I will send survivors to the nations, to Tarshish, Pul, and Lud, who draw the bow, to Tubal and Javan, to the coastlands far away, that have not heard my fame or seen my glory. And they shall declare my glory among the nations. And they shall bring all your brothers from all the nations as an offering to the Lord, on horses and in chariots and in litters and on mules and on dromedaries, to my holy mountain Jerusalem, says the Lord, just as the Israelites bring their grain offering in a clean vessel to the house of the Lord. *And some of them also I will take for priests and for Levites*, says the Lord. (Isa 66:18–21 ESV, emphasis mine)

This oracle implies that in this coming age when God will "declare his glory among the nations," the ministerial priesthood will be opened up to more than just the tribe of Levi. After describing how "all nations and tongues" will come and "see my glory," the Lord describes a great pilgrimage of foreigners to "my holy mountain Jerusalem," and these pilgrims will carry with them "all your brothers from the nations"—Isaiah's own kinsfolk, the people of Israel. Finally, God declares "some of them I will take for priests and for Levites," which means God will choose new "priests and Levites" either from the Israelites whom the Gentile pilgrims have brought back or perhaps from the Gentile pilgrims as well. It's not clear to whom, exactly, "some of *them*" refers. In either event, however, it is clear that the prohibition of the ministerial priestly role only to the Levites and sons of Aaron will be dropped, and God will choose "priests and Levites" from among the mixed group of Israelites and Gentiles that join the eschatological pilgrimage to Jerusalem.

Isaiah and the other prophets also speak about the return of the son of David in the last days. In their own lifetimes, the Davidic monarchy was in decline, and both Jeremiah and Ezekiel lived to see Jerusalem conquered and the king exiled. Nonetheless, the low estate of the Davidic monarchy would not last forever. Consider Isaiah 11:

> There shall come forth a shoot from the stump
>     of Jesse,
>         and a branch shall grow out of his roots.
>     And the Spirit of the Lord shall rest upon
>     him,
>         the spirit of wisdom and understanding,
>         the spirit of counsel and might,
>         the spirit of knowledge and the fear of the
>     Lord.
> And his delight shall be in the fear of the Lord.
>     (Isa 11:1–3)

Isaiah 9 reveals more about this son of David:

For to us a child is born,
>to us a son is given;
>and the government will be upon his shoulder,
>and his name will be called
>"Wonderful Counselor, Mighty God,
>Everlasting Father, Prince of Peace."
>Of the increase of his government and of
>peace
>>there will be no end,
>upon the throne of David, and over his kingdom,
>to establish it, and to uphold it
>with justice and with righteousness
from this time forth and for evermore. (Isa 9:6–7)

Other passages in Jeremiah and Ezekiel also take up this theme:

> But they shall serve the Lord their God and David their king, whom I will raise up for them. (Jer 30:9)

> My servant David shall be king over them; and they shall all have one shepherd. They shall follow my ordinances and be careful to observe my statutes. (Ezek 37:24)

These texts emphasize that David is coming back, and of course, David had the Melchizedekian priestly status.

In the Dead Sea Scrolls, we have a document known as 11QMelchizedek, written perhaps a century before the birth of Jesus. It's a short non-canonical prophecy in which an unknown author from the Essene movement predicted that Melchizedek would return at the end of ten jubilee cycles—that is, ten cycles of forty-nine years, for the Jubilee Year came every fiftieth. When he returned, Melchizedek would make atonement for God's people and announce an eschatological Jubilee Year. The original Jubilee Year described in Leviticus 25 was intended to remit monetary debts that Israelites may have had, and free them from any slavery into which they may have fallen. Not so the great Jubilee that Melchizedek would proclaim! His Jubilee would free God's elect from the *debt of sin* and from *slavery to Belial*, that is, Satan.

Is it a coincidence that in Luke 4:1–16 we read of Jesus preaching his first sermon in the synagogue of Nazareth, and he chooses as his text Isaiah 61:1–2, which describes one "anointed by the Spirit" to proclaim the "year of the Lord's favor"? This very text was cited in 11QMelchizedek and interpreted by the Essenes as a reference to Melchizedek and his supernatural Jubilee proclamation. Jesus announces that he is the fulfillment of this prophecy—quite a claim!—and he backs it up by almost immediately freeing a man from slavery to Satan (Luke 4:31–37) and forgiving another man of the debt of his sins (Luke 5:17–26). These were the very things the Essenes expected the end-times Melchizedek to do. Luke, then, is presenting Jesus to the Jews of his day as the promised "Melchizedek" that so many were anticipating. And Melchizedek is, of course, not just a *king* but a *priest*.

## SUMMARY

We began this chapter by looking into the Scriptures and finding that the priesthood continued from Isaac to the Exile. We saw Isaac build an altar and call on the name of the Lord. We also saw Isaac bless his son Jacob and so transfer to the next generation the blessing (Gen 26:27–29 and 28:1–4) he had received from his father Abraham (Gen 22:15–18), and therein fulfill the two essential priestly roles: sacrifice and blessing.

We observed Jacob also building altars (Gen 35:6) and setting up sacred pillars (Gen 35:14–15) and blessing his twelve sons (Gen 48:9–16; 49:1–28).

We showed that Joseph had a unique priestly role implicit in Genesis 45:8, where it says Joseph was "a father to Pharaoh"—meaning that Joseph consulted God on behalf of Pharaoh, offered prayers and sacrifices for him, and mediated God's blessing to him, casting Joseph in a priestly role.

We examined the continued development of the role of priests in Exodus, where God spoke of Israel as "my first-born son" (Exod 4:22). We saw God confer a priestly status upon the nation of Israel as a whole and establish the Israelites as a priestly people, since the primary reason God delivered them from slavery in Egypt was *for worship*.

We saw that, prior to the golden calf, the firstborn sons served in a capacity that we would recognize today as the *ministerial priesthood*. In this role, they took charge of the worship and sacrifice offered to God (Exodus 24:4–5). We then were able to identify a significant change to this original *priesthood of the firstborn* when Israel fell into idolatry and worshipped the molten calf (Exod 32): now the ministerial priestly status was transferred from the firstborn sons to the tribe of Levi, who took over responsibility for the sanctuary and for the liturgy (Num 3:12–13, 40–51).

We observed how this priestly role mediated God's presence to the other tribes and facilitated the forgiveness of sin, which allowed the people to stay in the covenant relationship with God (Lev 5). We also noted how the ancient Israelites had to confess their sins *to the priest* and the priest had to offer sacrifice on their behalf.

We were able to track the Levitical model of the priesthood continuing from the time of Moses until the time of David, and then we discovered that King David, though not a Levite, functioned as a priest. We looked at Samuel anointing him with oil "and from that day on, the spirit of the Lord rushed upon David" (1 Sam 16:13 NABRE) and observed examples of David's priestly role, such as eating the bread of Presence (1 Sam 21:1–6) and bringing the ark of the covenant to Jerusalem to unify the tribes and focus the national life on worship (2 Sam 6). We saw David dressed in a priestly garment of fine linen called an *ephod* (1 Chr 16:1–2; cf. 2 Sam 6:13–19), officiating at the altar by offering the sacrifice, blessing the people (fulfilling the second role of the priest), and that his sons in succession inherited a priestly status (Ps 110:1–4). We identified that the priesthood of David and his descendants originated not from the Levites but from Melchizedek (Ps 110).

We traced these two types of priesthood—the priesthood of the Levites and the priesthood of Melchizedek—and saw a further development of the priesthood introduced by the prophets who spoke of the coming of the Messianic age (Isa 40–66). We pointed to the priestly language in Isaiah 56 about foreigners, with the implication that they too would minister to the Lord in the temple in the coming age, that the ministerial priesthood would open up to more than just the tribe of Levi (Isa 66), and the restriction of the ministerial priestly role only to the Levites and sons of Aaron would be dropped. God would choose "priests and Levites" from among the mixed group of Israelites and Gentiles that join the eschatological pilgrimage to Jerusalem (Isa 66:21).

Finally, we looked at how Isaiah and the other prophets also spoke about the return of the son of David in the last days (Isa 9:6–7; 11:1–3; Jer 30:9; Ezek 37:24), recalling to mind that David enjoyed Melchizedekian priestly status. We also looked at Luke 4:1–16, where Jesus preached his first sermon in the synagogue of Nazareth and chose as his text Isaiah 61:1–2, which describes one "anointed by the Spirit" to proclaim the "year of the Lord's favor." We pointed out that this very text was cited in the Dead Sea Scrolls and interpreted by the Essenes as a reference to the priest-king Melchizedek and his supernatural Jubilee proclamation. We concluded that Jesus was announcing that he is the fulfillment of this prophecy: he is the promised "Melchizedek," the one who exercises both royal and sacerdotal power.

## Questions

1. How does the priesthood extend after Adam, Noah, and Abraham?

2. Describe the priestly role of Joseph in Genesis.

3. What is the connection between the priesthood and firstborn sons?

4. How can we understand what the terms "image" and "likeness" mean?

5. What are the different senses of the phrase "kingship of priests"?

6. How does the priesthood fall to the Levites? What are their responsibilities?

7. What evidence is there in Scripture of King David's priestly role?

8. Explain why it was possible for David's sons to be priests, though they were not Levites.

9. What prophesies—in Isaiah 55, 56, and elsewhere—are made about the New Covenant? How do they speak to a change in the Old Testament understanding of the priesthood?

10. What is the document known as 11QMelchizedek and how is it connected to the Gospel of Luke?

CHAPTER 3

# THE PRIESTHOOD IN THE NEW TESTAMENT

In the previous chapters we traced the priesthood through the Old Testament. Here, we examine it in the New Testament. The non-Catholic critique is that there is no ministerial priesthood in the New Testament era, that while we have a priesthood of all believers, the delineation of a ministerial priesthood of certain individuals is unscriptural. In more recent times, dissenting Catholic theologians also claim that there is no priestly concept of this kind in the Gospels, no concept of the apostolic succession of priests, and that the Mass is just a meal which does not require a priestly figure to celebrate it. This view has even trickled down into catechesis and religious education.

Of course, we'll see how those opinions don't hold up upon close examination.

## Priestly Themes in the Gospels

A first key scene to look at is the presentation of Jesus in the Temple:

> And when the time came for their purification according to the law of Moses, they brought him up to Jerusalem to present him to the Lord (as it is written in the law of the Lord, "Every male that opens the womb shall be called holy to the Lord") and to offer a sacrifice according to what is said in the law of the Lord, "a pair of turtledoves, or two young pigeons." (Luke 2:22–24)

At first glance this seems to be a fairly straightforward story, but there are several curious things happening here that one may not immediately recognize.

First, the passage says that they "brought him up to Jerusalem to present him to the Lord." This is not usually what you would go up to Jerusalem to do. When you had a firstborn son—one who "opens the womb"—you would usually go up to the Temple to *redeem* him (Exod 13:13). Why would you do this? Previously, we said that the first-born of Israel were consecrated in the Passover (Num 3:13), and according to Jewish tradition it was the first-born sons who helped out with the priestly duties with Moses prior to the sinful worship of the golden calf (Exod 24:5). After this, the firstborn lost their priestly duties, and these responsibilities were shifted to the Levites. We see this in the Book of Numbers:

> And the Lord said to Moses, "Take the Levites instead of all the first-born among the people of Israel, and the cattle of the Levites instead of their cattle; and the Levites shall be mine." (Num 3:44–45)

Thereafter, you had to redeem your firstborn at the price of an animal. The firstborn belonged to God, and, originally, you would have given your firstborn to the sanctuary to be raised as a priest. He would then be gone from you forever, meaning he would serve in the sanctuary as a priest for the rest of his life. Following the sin of worshiping the golden calf, the parent would have to buy their firstborn back from God for the price of an animal, and only after this redemption was he "laicized" or removed from his priestly duties. A Levite would take over his role and you could then bring your son home.

Now, let's return to the presentation of Jesus in the Temple. Looking at this scene we can see that it says nothing about redeeming Jesus and nothing about buying him back from his priestly role. This is significant, as I suspect that Luke did not believe that Jesus was ever *bought back from God*. Rather, Jesus was brought to the Temple and *presented*—because he was going to serve God in a priestly role. Recall that Luke quoted, "Every male that opens the womb shall be called holy to the Lord." This is the consecrated status of the firstborn son before he was bought back, redeemed, and replaced by a Levite (Exod 13:2). Luke doesn't quote the latter passages (after the calf) about having to be redeemed.

Instead, Luke says that Mary and Joseph "offer a sacrifice according to what is said in the law of the Lord, 'a pair of turtledoves, or two young pigeons.'" This is not the redemption sacrifice but is, rather, a sacrifice for the ritual purification of the mother (Lev 12:6–8). After the mother was completely healed, you would offer a sacrifice on her behalf that marked the return of what is called "ritual cleanliness," which meant she could participate in worship again. This sacrifice was offered on behalf of Mary, probably not because she underwent any physical injury, as is usual for women in childbirth, but most likely out of respect for custom—it might give scandal to friends and relatives if they did not offer the purification offering. In this passage, then, notice that Jesus is, strangely, *not redeemed.*

A similar thing happened to Samuel:

> And when she [Hannah] had weaned him, she took him up with her, along with a three-year-old bull, an ephah of flour, and a skin of wine; and she brought him to the house of the Lord at

Shiloh; and the child was young. Then they slew the bull, and they brought the child to Eli. And she said, "Oh, my lord! As you live, my lord, I am the woman who was standing here in your presence, praying to the Lord. For this child I prayed; and the Lord has granted me my petition which I made to him. Therefore I have lent him to the Lord; as long as he lives, he is lent to the Lord." (1 Sam 1:24–28)

Hannah brought Samuel to present him at the Temple, and he *stays*—he is not redeemed. Eli, Samuel's adoptive father, eventually dies, and Samuel becomes the high priest. Now, this may explain some of the reasons behind the finding of the child Jesus in the Temple, a passage that is full of curious features. Luke writes that Jesus said, "How is it that you sought me? Did you not know that I must be in my Father's house?" (Luke 2:49). In this scene, Jesus is essentially a model of Samuel. Perhaps Jesus knew he hadn't been redeemed as an baby, and when Mary and Joseph brought him to the Temple this second time, he thought it was now his time to fulfill his priestly duties, and that they were going to leave him just like Hannah left Samuel. The parallel here between Samuel and Jesus has been observed by Bible scholars,[1] some of whom

---

[1]  Richard Bauckham.

conclude that Luke is intentionally portraying Jesus—like Samuel—as the rare exception of an Israelite firstborn who is not redeemed but ends up fulfilling his consecration to God by serving as a priest.

Later in the Gospels, we have an interesting episode with the Apostles plucking grain on the Sabbath:

> At that time Jesus went through the grainfields on the sabbath; his disciples were hungry, and they began to pluck ears of grain and to eat. But when the Pharisees saw it, they said to him, "Look, your disciples are doing what is not lawful to do on the sabbath." He said to them, "Have you not read what David did, when he was hungry, and those who were with him: how he entered the house of God and ate the bread of the Presence, which it was not lawful for him to eat nor for those who were with him, but only for the priests? Or have you not read in the law how on the sabbath the priests in the temple profane the sabbath, and are guiltless? I tell you, something greater than the temple is here. And if you had known what this means, 'I desire mercy, and not sacrifice,' you would not have condemned the guiltless. For the Son of man is lord of the sabbath." (Matt 12:1–8 RSVCE)

Let's discuss the implications of the analogies that Jesus

draws here. First, he compares himself to David, who we know was "a priest forever according to the order of Melchizedek" (Ps 110:4). Then, he compares his Apostles to David's men in a situation where they performed a priestly act: they ate the bread of the Presence, which is a type of the Holy Eucharist. This is something that only priests were allowed to do. Jesus's logic here is that, as temple priests, he and his Apostles are allowed to work on the Sabbath. We tend to miss the significance of Jesus claiming priestly privileges for himself and his Apostles. He is establishing a new priesthood. This is especially clear to Jewish scholars who work on the Gospels. In his book *Jesus of Nazareth* (vol. 1), Pope Emeritus Benedict wanted to use this passage to support the concept of a New Testament priesthood. Knowing that if he made the argument himself, some readers would dismiss him as reading Catholic doctrine into Scripture, Pope Benedict simply quoted one of the most famous American rabbi-scholars of the twentieth century, Jacob Neusner, who comments on this passage:

> "He [Jesus] and his disciples may do on the Sabbath what they do because they stand in the place of the priests in the Temple."[2]

---

[2] Jacob Neusner, *A Rabbi Talks With Jesus* (Montreal: McGill-Queen's University Press, 2000), 83–84, quoted in Pope Benedict XVI, *Jesus of Nazareth: From the Baptism in the Jordan to the Transfiguration*, trans.

As is so often the case, the meaning of certain passages of the Gospels become clearer and better understood to those who are steeped in the Scriptures of Israel and the traditions of the Jewish people. Consider the conferral of the authority to "bind and loose" to Peter in Matthew 16:19, and to the Apostles as a group in Matthew 18:18. While contemporary Christians typically have no idea what these passages actually mean, we know that "binding and loosing" were terms that referred to the authority to make decisions about the interpretation of God's law and that this authority belonged to the priests under the Old Covenant.

We read in Deuteronomy 17 that if any of the people of Israel are faced with a problem in how to interpret or apply the laws of God, they are to go to the central sanctuary and there consult with the Levitical priests (Deut 17:8–9). The interpretation and decision of the Levitical priests had the same force and authority as God's law itself, such that whoever disobeyed the decision of the priest was to be put to death (Deut 17:10–13).

In time, the Jewish phrase used to describe this authority to interpret became "binding and loosing." "To bind" meant to forbid, and "to loose" meant to permit. Although the authority belonged to the priests, by the time Our Lord began his earthly ministry, the Pharisees had

Adrian J. Walker (New York: Doubleday, 2007), 108.

usurped this priestly role and practiced "binding and loosing" for the general populace of the Jewish people.[3] Jesus, however, gives this interpretive authority to Peter individually (Matt 16:19) and to the Apostles as a group (Matt 18:18). Everyone is familiar with these passages about "binding and loosing," but few Christian readers—even among Bible scholars—recognize that this was a *priestly prerogative* under the Mosaic Covenant (Deut 17:8–13) that Jesus now bestows on the *Apostles*, who will function as a new priesthood of the New Covenant.

Let's examine another important Gospel text that relates to Christ's priesthood: the cleansing of the Temple in the Gospel of John:

> The Jews then said to him, "What sign have you to show us for doing this?" Jesus answered them, "Destroy this temple, and in three days I will raise it up." The Jews then said, "It has taken forty-six years to build this temple, and will you raise it up in three days?" But he spoke of the temple of his body. When therefore he was raised from the dead, his disciples remembered that he had said

---

[3] See Flavius Josephus, *History of the Jewish War Against the Romans*, in *The Complete Works of Flavius Josephus*, trans. William Whiston (United Kingdom: e-artnow, 2018), 1.5. See also Rabbi Kaufmann Kohler, "Binding and Loosing," in the *Jewish Encyclopedia*, available here: http://www.jewishencyclopedia.com/articles/3307-binding-and-loosing.

this; and they believed the Scripture and the word which Jesus had spoken. (John 2:18–22)

Notice that John explains that Jesus "spoke of the temple of his body." This is an interesting statement. If we look at this from a historical-cultural background, we can find a few precedents in Judaism for likening a man's body to a temple. Let's look first at the Wisdom of Solomon, which speaks of the clothing of the high priest in the following way: "For upon his long robe the whole world was depicted, and the glories of the fathers were engraved on the four rows of stones, and thy majesty on the diadem upon his head" (Wis 18:24).

So we see that the cosmos was depicted on the robe of the high priest. Remember earlier we established that the cosmos was a macro-temple. So the high priest would enter the Jerusalem temple with the macro-temple of the cosmos depicted on his body. His body is, symbolically, the cosmic temple. So here in John 2:18–22 when Jesus speaks of his own body as a temple, we recognize that Jesus is the true high priest, the cosmic man. He's the new Adam coming in on behalf of the temple cosmos and offering worship to God. He is the man whose body represents the cosmic temple.

Further confirmation of this concept comes from Philo, a philosopher from Alexandria in Egypt who was roughly contemporary to St. Paul. In his *Life of Moses*, he says, "Then [Moses] gave [the priests] their sacred vestments, giving to his brother [Aaron, the high priest] the robe which reached down to his feet, and the mantle which covered his shoulders, as a sort of breast-plate, being an embroidered robe, adorned with all kinds of figures, and a *representation of the universe.*"[4] If we follow Philo's biography of Moses further, he says that the high priest "represents the world" and is a "microcosm."[5]

Josephus, the famous Jewish historian who lived through the destruction of Jerusalem, says much the same, writing, "For if anyone do but consider the fabric of the tabernacle, and take a view of the garments of the high priest, and of those vessels which we make use of in our sacred ministration, he will find . . . they were every one made in way of imitation and representation of the universe."[6] Again, we have a comparison between the temple and the body, a concept of the high priest that Jesus applies to himself.

Now, let's return to the New Testament and look at the crucifixion of the Lord in the Gospel of John. John mentions that the tunic Jesus wore was "without seam, woven from top to bottom" (John 19:23). This is why the

---

[4] Philo Judaeus, *On the Life of Moses, II*, in *The Works of Philo Judaeus, vol. II*, trans. Charles Duke Yonge (Ontario, Canada: Devoted Publishing, 2017), 143.

[5] Philo, *Life of Moses*, 135.

[6] Flavius Josephus, *Jewish Antiquities*, trans. William Whiston (Ware, Hertfordshire: Wordsworth Editions Limited, 2006), 3:180.

Roman soldiers had to cast lots for it (see John 19:24). In ancient Jewish times, such a tunic was extremely rare. Weaving a garment like this was a challenge and took a lot of time, effort, and forethought. It was not something that was normally done. Significantly, the only seamless garment for which we have an historical record from this time period was the robe of the high priest. According to Josephus, "The high priest is indeed adorned with . . . a vestment of a blue color. This also is a long robe, reaching to his feet. . . . Now this vesture was not composed of two pieces, nor was it sewed together upon the shoulders and the sides, but *it was one long vestment so woven as to have an aperture for the neck.*"[7] So we can see that Jesus's seamless tunic was a symbol of his high priestly role.

Of course, few Christians would dispute that Jesus is our high priest in the New Covenant. But what about the disciples? Do they participate at all in this priestly role of Christ? We've already seen indications that they do, from texts like Matthew 12:1–8, 16:19, and 18:18. But we also see indications in the Gospel of John. Let's back up before the crucifixion and look at the foot washing of the disciples in the Upper Room:

> Now before the feast of the Passover, when Jesus
> knew that his hour had come to depart out of this

---

[7] Josephus, *Jewish Antiquities*, 3:159–161.

world to the Father, having loved his own who were in the world, he loved them to the end. And during supper, when the devil had already put it into the heart of Judas Iscariot, Simon's son, to betray him, Jesus, knowing that the Father had given all things into his hands, and that he had come from God and was going to God, rose from supper, laid aside his garments, and tied a towel around himself. Then he poured water into a basin, and began to wash the disciples' feet, and to wipe them with the towel that was tied around him. He came to Simon Peter; and Peter said to him, "Lord, do you wash my feet?" Jesus answered him, "What I am doing you do not know now, but afterward you will understand." Peter said to him, "You shall never wash my feet." Jesus answered him, "If I do not wash you, you have no part in me." Simon Peter said to him, "Lord, not my feet only but also my hands and my head!" Jesus said to him, "He who has bathed does not need to wash, except for his feet, but he is clean all over; and you are clean, but not all of you." (John 13:1–10)

We see here that Jesus laid aside his garments, poured water, and began to wash the disciples' feet. If we revisit Exodus, we discover that the priests had to wash their feet before entering the sanctuary and performing any kind of ministerial duty (Exod 30:19–21). The similarity between Jesus's actions and those of the priests in Exodus is striking, especially because this foot washing occurs before the institution of the Eucharist. At this meal, Jesus says, "This is my body which is given for you. Do this in remembrance of me. . . . This chalice which is poured out for you is the new covenant in my blood" (Luke 22:19–20). Note that Jesus says, "Do this in remembrance of me." He is telling his disciples to do this as a *memorial*. The word "memorial" is a liturgical term: it was the name of a grain sacrifice that was regularly offered to God in the Temple to "remind" God of the covenant (we would say, "to renew" the covenant).[8] Returning to the washing of feet, we can now see that Jesus is about to commission his disciples to be priests of the new-covenant "memorial" sacrifice of the Eucharist, and he is preparing them by washing their feet, just as was required in the Old Covenant.

Peter's protest in this passage is also significant. Peter says, "You shall never wash my feet." Jesus replies, "If I do not wash you, you have no part in me," and then Peter says, "Lord, not my feet only but also my hands and my head!" Let's examine Jesus's reply further. In Greek, the

---

[8]  Lev 6:14, 24:7. In Greek, the name for this "memorial sacrifice" was *anamnesis*, the same word used in the Institution Narratives of the Gospels. Two Psalms were designated to be sung for this sacrifice: see the headings of Pss 37 and 69 in the LXX (= Pss 38 & 70 in Hebrew and English).

word for "part" or "portion" is *meris*, and it is almost exclusively priestly. Let's look at the Book of Numbers:

> And the Lord said to Aaron, "You shall have no inheritance in their land, neither shall you have any portion among them; I am your portion and your inheritance among the people of Israel. To the Levites I have given every tithe in Israel for an inheritance, in return for their service which they serve, their service in the tent of meeting" (Num 18:20–21).

Priests have no *meris*, no portion among Israel; rather, the Lord says that he is their *meris*, their portion. All the other tribes received land as their portion, but the priesthood received God Himself. When Jesus replies to Peter, "If I do not wash you, you have no part in me," he is saying that Peter's "part" or inheritance, like that of the Old Testament priesthood, will be himself alone—that is, God alone.

What else in the New Testament reflects priesthood concepts? Let's look to what is called the High Priestly Prayer in the Gospel of John (17:1–26). This famous prayer, the longest recorded prayer of Jesus in the New Testament, begins with Jesus praying to his Father on his own behalf: "Father, the hour has come; glorify your Son that the Son may glorify you, since you have given him power over all flesh, to give eternal life to all whom you have given him" (John 17:1–2). He continues to pray for himself until verse six, which starts a new section where he begins praying for the Apostles. He says, "I have manifested your name to the men whom you gave me out of the world; they were yours, and you gave them to me, and they have kept your word" (John 17:6). Jesus continues to pray for the Apostles until verse 20. Then, he switches to praying for all those who will believe through the word of the Apostles, that is to say, the Church. He continues to pray for the entire Church all the way to the end of the chapter.

Thus, when we step back from this passage in John and look at the prayer overall, we can see that Jesus prays first for himself (vv. 1–5), then for the Apostles (vv. 6–20), and then for the entire Church (vv. 20–26). Scholars have noted that this structure follows the pattern of the "Day of Atonement," the highest holy day of the Jewish liturgical calendar, known among the Jews as Yom Kippur. On this day, the high priest would enter into the Holy of Holies and make atonement for himself, then for his family (i.e., the rest of the priests), and then for the entire people of God. We can see this in Leviticus:

> There shall be no man in the tent of meeting
> when he enters to make atonement in the holy
> place until he comes out and has made atonement

for himself and for his house and for all the assembly of Israel. (Lev 16:17)

The High Priestly Prayer is clearly parallel in structure to the prayer made during the Day of Atonement, which is why scholars call it "the High Priestly Prayer." One of the themes of this prayer is the "manifestation of the name." Jesus says that he has "manifested thy name." He has revealed God's Name to the Apostles. Historically, the Day of Atonement was the only day of the year on which anyone would actually pronounce the divine name "YHWH." During the prayers of the Day of Atonement liturgy, the name of the Lord was invoked frequently. But on this day, the high priest would not substitute the title "the Lord" but would actually pronounce the phonetics of the divine name "YHWH"—and every time he pronounced the divine name, everyone gathered before him would fall down in reverence.[9] So the "manifestation of the name" is yet another motif that connects Jesus' High Priestly Prayer with the Day of Atonement and the role of the high priest himself.

We can see a further connection to the revelation of the divine name later in John, when Jesus and his Apostles are in the Garden of Gethsemane: "Then Jesus, knowing all that was to befall him, came forward and said to them,

---

[9]  See the Mishnah, tractate Yoma 6:1; cf. Sirach 50:20–21.

'Whom do you seek?' They answered, 'Jesus of Nazareth.' Jesus said to them, 'I AM.' Judas, who betrayed him, was standing with them. When he said to them, 'I AM,' they drew back and fell to the ground" (John 18:4–6, my translation). Unwittingly, the crowd that arrives to arrest Jesus fulfills the duty of the congregation at the Day of Atonement to prostrate themselves at the pronunciation of the divine name, which is "I AM" (Exod 3:14).

Returning to John 17, we observe that Jesus demonstrates his own priestly role through its similarities to the role of the high priest on the Day of Atonement. Now, in his prayer, Jesus also requests that his Apostles be included in this priestly role. He says: "Sanctify them in the truth; your word is truth. As you sent me into the world, so I have sent them into the world. And for their sake I consecrate myself, that they also may be consecrated in truth" (John 17:17–19).

In Greek, the word "sanctify" or "consecrate" is *hagiazo*. In the Greek translation of the Old Testament (the LXX), the vast majority of the cases where *hagiazo* is applied to male human beings are describing men being ordained as priests. For example, Exodus says, "And you shall put them upon Aaron your brother, and upon his sons with him, and shall anoint them and ordain them and *consecrate* [*hagiazo*] them, that they may serve me as priests" (Exod 28:41).

Likewise, Leviticus notes, "The priest who is chief among his brethren, upon whose head the anointing oil is poured, and who has been *consecrated* [*hagiazo*] to wear the garments, shall not let the hair on his head hang loose, nor rend his clothes" (Lev 21:10).

Jesus has *consecrated himself* as a priest, and he prays that his Father will *consecrate* his Apostles as well. The culmination of the consecration of the Apostles in the Gospel of John arrives on Easter Sunday, when Jesus appears to the Eleven and bestows on them the sanctifying power of the Holy Spirit: "He breathed on them and said to them, 'Receive the Holy Spirit. Whose sins you forgive are forgiven them. Whose sins you retain are retained'" (John 20:22–23). Whose duty was it to make decisions about "forgiving" or "retaining" sins in the Old Covenant?

> If anyone sins ... when he realizes his guilt ... and *confesses the sin he has committed*, he shall bring to the Lord as his compensation for the sin that he has committed . . . a sin offering. And *the priest* shall make atonement for him for his sin . . . and *he shall be forgiven.* (Lev 5:1–13 ESV, emphasis mine)

And the sinner confesses the sin he has committed to the priest (Lev 5:5) because the priest has the responsibility to ensure that the Israelite penitent brings the proper sacrifice commensurate with his wealth and the gravity of his sin, and that it is offered in the proper way. If an Israelite committed some grave offense and appeared at the sanctuary with a sacrifice of little worth, perhaps a lame animal or a pair of pigeons, the priest had the responsibility to refuse atonement and forgiveness, and send the penitent back to acquire the appropriate sacrifice—thus "retaining" his sin at least temporarily. Thus, receiving confession and mediating forgiveness—not to mention offering sacrifice!—were priestly roles in the Old Testament. And in John 20:22–23, Jesus bestows that priestly role on the Apostles.

Of course, offering sacrifice was central to the priestly ministry of mediating forgiveness. To see the Apostles' priestly role of sacrifice, let's turn now from the Gospel of John to the Synoptic Gospels and examine the accounts of the Last Supper itself, that is, the institution of the Eucharist.

According to Matthew, Jesus "took a chalice, and when he had given thanks he gave it to them, saying, 'Drink of it, all of you; for this is my blood of the covenant, which is poured out for many for the forgiveness of sins'" (Matt 26:27–28).

This phrase is very significant: "blood of the covenant." We might think that this would be a common phrase in the Bible, but it actually isn't. The exact phrase, "blood of the covenant," occurs in only one place in the Old Testament, back in Exodus when Moses is establishing the Sinai covenant for the first time.[10] In this passage, God has just spoken the Ten Commandments from Mount Sinai and Moses has slaughtered oxen as a sacrifice. Moses then sprinkles the altar with blood and turns to the people, saying, "Behold the blood of the covenant which the Lord has made with you in accordance with all these words" (Exod 24:8) as he dashes blood upon them. Blood only becomes available after one has slain an animal, and in a sacred context after one has *sacrificed* the animal. Covenant rituals often employed blood, which was both a symbol of the kinship bond being formed by the covenant, as well as the curse of death should one party violate the terms of the covenant. The blood for the covenant-making rite always came from a sacrifice, as is reflected in Psalm 50:5: "Gather to me my faithful ones, who have made a covenant with me by sacrifice!" So Our Lord's very words "the blood of the covenant" also imply that a sacrifice has taken place.

Indeed, Jesus's use of the phrase "this is my blood of the covenant" is theologically supercharged. Essentially, Jesus is claiming to be redoing Sinai, not with animal blood but with his own blood. The phrase "blood of the covenant" refers back to the Exodus account of the mak-

---

[10] Exodus 24:8. In Zech 9:11, there is an allusion to Exod 24:8, but the phrase used is "the blood of *your* covenant."

ing of the Sinai covenant, where Moses had acted in a priestly role.

This is significant. Typically, when people debate the divinity of Christ, they point to the passages when John says, "The Word was with God, and the Word was God" (John 1:1), or when Thomas falls down and says, "My Lord and my God!" (John 20:28). People who want to disprove Christ's divinity think that if they can debunk these passages, that will prove that Jesus is not divine.

Debunking those passages does not disprove Christ's divinity. Everything that Jesus claims throughout the Gospels—that he and his disciples outrank David in his priestly role, that he is greater than the Temple, and again, here, that he is redoing Sinai with his own blood—is astounding! Everything he does proclaims his divinity!

For Jews, there was no one in the universe higher in status than Moses and no event in history higher in status than the making of the covenant at Sinai. For Jesus to claim to be redoing and even outdoing Moses implies that Jesus is the only person who outranks Moses: God Himself! These implications were not lost on Jesus' contemporaries. Indeed, on more than one occasion in the Gospel of John, the Jews of Jesus' day believed that his claims were outrageous, that either what Jesus said was true or he was essentially pathologically arrogant and even blasphemous (John 8:57–59; 10:33).

At the Last Supper, Jesus also said that his blood is "poured out for many for the forgiveness of sins" (Matt 26:28). We have seen that the forgiveness of sins in the Old Testament was accomplished by the ministry of the priests (Lev 5:1–13), so we understand that Jesus is offering his own blood for the forgiveness of sins. This is very clearly a priestly action. It also draws on imagery from the famous prophecy of Isaiah 53, which describes the "servant of the Lord" as a priestly figure who is also the sacrificial victim (Isa 53:10–12).

In his First Letter to the Corinthians, St. Paul records a little bit more about this incident: "For I received from the Lord what I also delivered to you, that the Lord Jesus on the night when he was betrayed took bread, and when he had given thanks, he broke it, and said, "This is my body which is for you. Do this in remembrance of me" (1 Cor 11:23–24). Here Paul informs us that Jesus commissioned the Apostles to perform this act as a *continual event.*

Let's examine the phrase, "in remembrance," or in the Greek *anamnesis.* This Greek word calls to mind the Old Testament sacrificial system that included a remembrance or memorial sacrifice, an *anamnesis* offering. In fact, two psalms (Pss 38 and 70) were written to be chanted during this sacrifice, and in the Septuagint or LXX, the ancient Greek translation of the Old Testament sometimes used by Our Lord and the Apostles, these psalms are entitled, "For the *anamnesis*," that is, for the memorial offering.[11] Likewise, Jesus' words as recorded in the Gospels and First Corinthians could be translated, "Do this as *my* memorial offering." Although it might accompany an animal sacrifice, the memorial offering consisted only of flour or grain, not meat.[12] This is significant, as the Eucharist is the bloodless sacrifice that participates in the bloody sacrifice of Jesus. Christ offered his body on the cross, and thereafter we do the "memorial sacrifice," which consists of the grain which is typified already in the Old Testament system. Thus the phrase "do this as my *anamnesis*" is fraught with the connotations of the priestly sacrifice of the memorial offering. At the Last Supper, Jesus is authorizing the Apostles to continue his Moses-like, priestly, sacrificial, covenant-establishing sacrifice.

## What Kind of Priest Is Jesus?

We have established that there are strong priestly themes in the Gospels. Now, let us address the question: What kind of priest is Jesus? He is clearly not a priest from the tribe of Levi, so how can he actually be a priest? Although that may not be much of an issue for us today, this was a

---

[11] The psalms are numbered differently in the LXX, so see the titles of LXX Psalms 37 and 69.

[12] Leviticus 2:16; 5:12; 6:15; 24:7.

complicated question for the first-century Jews. We find our answer in the Letter to the Hebrews: Jesus is a priest after the order of Melchizedek. For example, in one of the key passages in the Letter to the Hebrews, we read:

> For this Melchizedek, king of Salem, priest of the Most High God, met Abraham returning from the slaughter of the kings and blessed him; and to him Abraham apportioned a tenth part of everything. He is first, by translation of his name, king of righteousness, and then he is also king of Salem, that is, king of peace. He is without father or mother or genealogy, and has neither beginning of days nor end of life, but resembling the Son of God he continues a priest for ever. (Heb 7:1–3)

This strange verse is usually interpreted as follows: Melchizedek has a "cameo" role in the Bible. He enters for one scene and then we never see him again. We never find out who his father or mother was, and we never hear about his death. So, according to the usual interpretation, the author of the Letter to the Hebrews is saying that because we don't hear anything in Scripture about Melchizedek's ancestry and we don't hear about his death, *therefore*, he had no parents and he never died, and that makes him like Jesus!

There are a number of different problems with this interpretation.

First of all, there are many people in Scripture whose ancestors, fathers, and mothers are not recorded, such as Rahab's parents. Does that make her a priest forever like Jesus? That doesn't make much sense. Furthermore, Jesus *did* have parents, and he *did* have a genealogy—two of them, in fact! (Matt 1; Luke 3). Not only does Jesus have multiple genealogies, an adopted father, and a natural mother, but we also know that he had a birthdate (Christmas) and an end of life (Good Friday).

Then, what's the analogy between Melchizedek and Jesus? We have to look for something deeper. St. Paul was trying to communicate something here, but the usual modern interpretation simply doesn't make sense.

The key to understanding this passage is to know the requirements of the Levitical priesthood in the time of Jesus.[13] In first-century Israel, a Levite who wanted to go serve in the Temple (which was his ancestral privilege) had to demonstrate his genealogy on *both* his father's and mother's sides. He had to show who his father and mother were and produce documentation that both his father and mother were Levites at least four generations back on both sides. He could not have any intermarriage. Then, once he became a priest, his service was limited. He began his days as a priest at age thirty, his mandatory retirement

---

[13] On this, see Scott Hahn, *Kinship by Covenant* (New Haven: Yale, 2009), 278-307.

was age fifty, and so he was eligible for a twenty-year career as a priest.[14]

Let's return to the passage from the Letter to the Hebrews in which St. Paul says that Melchizedek is: "without father or mother or genealogy, and has neither beginning of days nor end of life." Now, if you insert the word "Levitical" into this verse, which is appropriate in this context, the passage starts to make sense. Melchizedek is without a *Levitical* father or *Levitical* mother or *Levitical* genealogy; he has neither a *Levitical* "beginning of days" nor a *Levitical* "end of life." He resembles "the Son of God [and] he continues a priest for ever." "For ever" is too strong a translation of the Greek;[15] rather, we can understand that he is a priest "perpetually." It means that Melchizedek was a lifelong priest and didn't have a mandatory retirement age of fifty like the Levites did.

Now we can see what St. Paul was trying to say in this passage. He was attempting to explain where in the Bible you can find a priest who doesn't have any kind of connection to the Levites. St. Paul wants us to look at Melchizedek, as he doesn't have any of those Levitical requirements and he doesn't fall under Levitical legislation.

Jesus is a priest like him in many ways. According to Jewish tradition they are linked by royal succession.

---

[14] Num 4:3, 23, 30, 35, 39, 43, 47.
[15] Greek *eis to diênekes*, lit. "unto perpetuity."

Melchizedek was known as the king of "Salem," the ancient name of "Jerusalem." Later, Jesus's ancestor David became king of Jerusalem (2 Sam 5:6–10) and entered into Melchizedekian succession, which passed down the royal line (2 Sam 8:18). This is what Psalm 110:4 means when it says of the Davidic king: "You are a priest forever, according to the order of Melchizedek." Jesus was the royal son of David, and so, by typology as well as ancestry, Jesus inherits this "Melchizedekian" priesthood.

We now see that Jesus is a priest forever after the order Melchizedek, like his father David. In Jewish tradition, Melchizedek's priesthood had been passed down from father to the firstborn son, all the way from Adam to Melchizedek himself. Recall that Adam was understood to exercise a priestly role in the Garden of Eden, as we saw earlier in our discussion. As we follow the genealogies of Genesis, we see that the line of patriarchs from Adam all the way to Shem is inheriting the priesthood. Furthermore, Jewish tradition identified Melchizedek with Shem. Seeing that Shem lives into the days of Abraham, and noticing that Melchizedek seems to be superior to Abraham and blesses Abraham (Gen 14:18–20), the ancient Jews raised the question: "Who on earth was alive in the days of Abraham and would be superior to him?" The logical answer was Shem. Already in many of the earliest commentaries on Scripture in the Jewish tradition,

Melchizedek is identified as Shem.[16]

Melchizedek's priesthood is a priesthood of the first-born son, inherited by way of a chain of fathers and first-born sons going back to Adam, which is the priesthood that we as Christians participate in. Hebrews 12:22–24 says:

> But you have come to Mount Zion and to the city of the living God, the heavenly Jerusalem, and to innumerable angels in festal gathering, and to the assembly [lit. "church"] of the *first-born* who are enrolled in heaven, and to a judge who is God of all, and to the spirits of just men made perfect, and to Jesus, the mediator of a new covenant, and to the sprinkled blood that speaks more graciously than the blood of Abel. (emphasis mine)

Note that "the heavenly Jerusalem" is a poetic description of the Church and that the "assembly [literally *ecclesia* or 'church'] of the first-born" refers to the concept of the firstborn of Israel, those who originally had priestly status (Exod 13:3).

## COMMON OR ROYAL PRIESTHOOD OF CHRISTIANS

We have discussed several instances where the concept of priesthood is apparent in the New Testament. Now let's

---

[16] Hahn, *Kinship*, 299-300.

delve into the ways that we participate, as Christians, in Christ's priesthood. There are two modes of participation in Christ's priesthood: the common (or royal) and the ministerial. Let's first look at the common priesthood, the basic priesthood of all Christians.

We see the concept of the common priesthood reflected in several important places in the New Testament, including the famous passage from Romans: "I appeal to you therefore, brethren, by the mercies of God, to present your bodies as a living sacrifice, holy and acceptable to God, which is your spiritual worship" (Rom 12:1).

St. Paul uses priestly language in this passage—"present," "sacrifice," "holy and acceptable," "worship"—all come from the sphere of the temple and priestly service. We Christians are a priesthood and we have a sacrifice to offer—the sacrifice of our bodies. Offering our bodies as living sacrifices is probably not just referring to physical mortifications, but the word "bodies" is most likely a form of *metonymy*[17] that symbolizes our entire lives.

The body-as-sacrifice is a reality that goes back to Adam's original priesthood. Recall that Adam's potential sacrifice was his whole self, which—ultimately—he wasn't willing to offer to defend his bride. Now that we are baptized into the new Adam, we are called to offer what

---

[17] A literary device where a thing or concept is represented by the name of something closely associated with it, for example, "Those lands belong to the crown" or "The White House made that decision."

Adam refused—our very selves. St. Paul's statement reflects a priestly concept of the whole people of God. This idea isn't limited to St. Paul. St. Peter, likewise, says to the Church: "But you are a chosen race, a royal priesthood, a holy nation, God's own people, that you may declare the wonderful deeds of him who called you out of darkness into his marvelous light" (1 Pet 2:9).

Here, St. Peter applies to the Church terms that were originally applied to the nation of Israel at Sinai. More specifically, they were the roles that God promised Israel if they would keep the covenant:

> "Now therefore, if you will obey my voice and keep my covenant, you shall be my own possession among all peoples; for all the earth is mine, and you shall be to me a kingdom of priests and a holy nation. These are the words which you shall speak to the children of Israel" (Exod 19:5–6).

This status and these roles were offered to the people of Israel, but in the end they rejected the offer by worshiping the golden calf and then by rebelling ten times in the wilderness (Exod 32:1–6; Num 14:22). St. Peter is saying that the offer rejected by Israel is now actualized in the Church. Members of the Church really are a "chosen race, a royal priesthood."

Oftentimes Catholics think of this common priesthood,

or what is also called the "priesthood of all believers," as a Protestant doctrine; however, Protestants got this doctrine from the Church Fathers, and the Fathers got it from Scripture itself. So it's also part of Catholic doctrine. St. Peter Chrysologus, who wrote between AD 380–450—over one thousand years before Luther—says: "Listen now to what the Apostle urges us to do. I appeal to you, he says, to present your bodies as a living sacrifice. By this exhortation of his, Paul has raised all men to priestly status." St. Peter Chrysologus recognized the connotations of the Greek and saw right away what St. Paul is doing. The passage continues:

> How marvelous is the priesthood of the Christian, for he is both the victim that is offered on his own behalf, and the priest who makes the offering. He does not need to go beyond himself to seek what he is to immolate to God: with himself and in himself he brings the sacrifice he is to offer God for himself. The victim remains and the priest remains, always one and the same. Immolated, the victim still lives: the priest who immolates cannot kill. Truly it is an amazing sacrifice in which a body is offered without being slain and blood is offered without being shed.[18]

Likewise, St. Augustine says: "Just as we call all the baptized

---

[18] Peter Chrysologus, Sermon 108 (PL 52:499–500), in *The Liturgy of the Hours,* Tuesday of the Fourth Week of Easter, Office of Readings, 2nd Reading.

Christians, in virtue of the one chrism, so we also call all of them priests, because they are members of the one priest."[19] The Catechism of the Catholic Church also teaches this:

> The whole Church is a priestly people. Through Baptism all the faithful share in the priesthood of Christ. This participation is called the "common priesthood of the faithful." Based on this common priesthood and ordered to its service, there exists another participation in the mission of Christ: the ministry conferred by the sacrament of Holy Orders, where the task is to serve in the name and in the person of Christ the Head in the midst of the community. (CCC 1591)

Even the priestly service of ministerial priests is based on the foundation of their Baptism. They are common priests *first*, they *remain* common priests, and then, in addition, they take on this ministerial priesthood.

Ministerial priests exist to help the rest of us do what God has called us to do. They feed us the sacraments so we have a spiritual power to make our bodies a "living sacrifice." We don't exist for them; rather, they exist for us, to feed us and nourish us for our mission. Our mission

---

[19] St. Augustine of Hippo, *City of God*, XX:10, quoted in Monsignor Fernando Ocáriz, "Letter from the Prelate (November 2009)," https://opusdei.org/en-us/document/letter-from-the-prelate-november-2009/.

is outside the church door in the world. A great modern saint who spent his life developing a path to holiness for lay people, St. Josemaría Escrivá, writes:

> All Christians, without exception, have been made priests of our lives, "to offer spiritual sacrifices acceptable to God through Jesus Christ" (1 Pet 2:5). Everything we do can be an expression of our obedience to God's will and so perpetuate the mission of the God-man.[20]

In another place, he says,

> With this priestly soul, which I ask God to grant all of you, you have to see to it that in the midst of your daily occupations, your entire life is turned into a continual praise of God: constant prayer and reparation, petition and sacrifice for all mankind. And all of this in intimate and assiduous union with Christ Jesus, in the Holy Sacrifice of the Altar.[21]

I had a confessor some years ago to whom I would go for spiritual direction. In these direction sessions I would go on talking for quite some time about all the various

---

[20] Josemaría Escrivá, *Christ is Passing By*, §96, quoted in Ocáriz, "Letter from the Prelate (November 2009)."

[21] Josemaría Escrivá, *Letter of March 28, 1955*, §4, quoted in Ocáriz, "Letter from the Prelate (November 2009)."

contradictions I was experiencing in my life, and he would always tell me, "John, offer these things with your priestly soul." I always thought that was a striking image. I'd imagine a little version of myself with a Roman collar, sitting right over my heart, physically lifting things up with two hands like a priest elevates the Host at Mass. It's a funny mental image—a mini-me in a Roman collar—but there is a spiritual truth there. We all, both men and women, have an inner priest which we have to let out.

There is a place in the Mass where this "priestly soul" of the lay faithful is symbolically represented. It is the liturgical act of offering the gifts. The Roman Missal says: "It is desirable that the faithful manifest their participation in the oblation by bringing forward either bread and wine for the celebration of the Eucharist, or other gifts, for the necessities of the Church and the poor."[22]

This liturgical act of bringing forward the gifts represents how the common priesthood and the ministerial priesthood together offer worship to God. The unconsecrated bread and wine that you and I might bring forward in Mass and hand over to the ministerial priest represent our bodies as a living sacrifice. They represent our whole lives and all that we do, everything from changing diapers

---

[22] The Roman Missal. In Latin: *Expedit ut fideles participationem suam oblatione manifestent, afferendo sive panem et vinum ad Eucharistiae celebrationem, sive alia dona, quibus necessitatibus Ecclesiae et pauperum subveniatur.*

to paying bills to going to work. Essentially, all the events of our daily lives are like the unconsecrated bread and wine. We bring the raw matter of our lives up to ministerial priest, and he takes it and calls the Holy Spirit down upon it, and it becomes the Body of Christ. This shows how our sacrifice is being united to Christ's. Recall that St. Josemaría said that our personal sacrifices should be offered "in intimate and assiduous union with Christ Jesus in the Holy Sacrifice of the Altar."[23] Through the prayers and actions of the ministerial priest, the sacrifice of our daily lives in the common world is united to the Eucharistic sacrifice, and together, they become the sacrifice of Christ.

So, the ministerial priest and the common priest have to work together to offer the Eucharistic sacrifice. In a sense, what would the ministerial priesthood do without the common priesthood to bring forward the raw matter of the world? On the other hand, what would we common priests do if we didn't have the ministerial priesthood to call down the Holy Spirit upon these gifts to sanctify our offerings?

This represents a dynamic that characterizes not just the Eucharistic liturgy but the whole Christian life. It is a dynamic between the common priesthood and the minis-

---

[23] Josemaría Escrivá, *Letter of March 28, 1955*, §4, quoted in Monsignor Fernando Ocáriz, "Letter from the Prelate (November 2009)," https://opusdei.org/en-us/document/letter-from-the-prelate-november-2009/.

terial priesthood. The ministerial priests exist to sanctify what the common priests are doing and to make it a perfect offering.

When the celebrant at Mass says, *Orate, fratres, ut meum ac vestrum sacrificium acceptabile fiat apud Deum Patrem omnipotentem* ("Pray, Brethren, that my sacrifice and yours become acceptable to God the Father Almighty"), the Latin phrase *meum ac vestrum sacrificium* ("my sacrifice and yours") emphasizes this complementarity between the common priesthood that sacrifices the daily matter of this world and the celebrant's own sacramental sacrifice.

The common priesthood of every Christian does not mean that we are "deputy priests," that is, deputy ministerial priests. We are not trying to do the same thing as the ministerial priesthood on a lower level. Rather, we express our priesthood not primarily in the liturgy but out in the world, through living an ordinary life with extraordinary holiness.

When some people think about the priesthood of all believers, they understand this to mean that they should take on a bigger liturgical role, as a lector or an extraordinary minister of the Eucharist, perhaps, to express their common priesthood. While it is certainly good to want to be involved in their parish, this interpretation is incorrect. The common priest is to serve out in the world, and the liturgy is the domain of the ministerial priesthood. Lay people shouldn't try to do what clergy are doing at a lower level by adopting some subordinate role in the celebration of Mass. Instead, we should be going to our offices and sanctifying the cubicle, the water cooler, the telephone, our iPads, or whatever tools we use to do our work. We should try to sanctify what's called the *temporal order*—ordinary society.

In the Church we have some members arguing for the ordination of men and women as an expression of the common priesthood. This is a misguided application because the realm of the common priesthood is in the world, in politics, in business, in education, and so on. Professors exercise their common priesthood by bringing the light of Christ to their peers and students. They do this with excellence, and, where appropriate, they show people how their discipline points to a transcendent reality and ultimately to Christ. Those who work in politics are in an excellent position to work for the common good, to uphold the moral order and, again, where appropriate, point to how the political world needs completion in God. We are to exercise our common priesthood by bringing Christ to secular society.

With the nature of our common priesthood correctly understood, let's now discuss the essential elements of a priestly character.

The first element is prayer. It is important to develop

the habit of prayer, even constant prayer, throughout the day. We should have both vocal prayer, like the Rosary or Divine Mercy Chaplet, as well as *mental prayer*, the traditional term in the Catholic spiritual tradition for an interior conversation with God in our heart, which some call "free prayer," "conversational prayer," or "meditation." Every Catholic can and should practice some form of mental prayer, since it is one of the most important means for developing a personal and intimate relationship with God.

The next element of a priestly character is mortification. Even the laity have to live ascetic lives and practice at least small mortifications. Obviously, we can't fast strenuously because we have other obligations. For example, if a dad is irritable because he hasn't eaten for two days and then gets angry with his children because he's irritable, it undermines the whole purpose of fasting. Rather than fasting from all food, someone could simply skip butter or condiments and be mortified through acts of self-denial without lacking nourishment. As St. Josemaría recommended: "Choose mortifications that don't mortify others."[24]

The third element of a priestly character is excellent performance in our work. The Old Testament gives instructions for the offering of sacrifices, saying, "You shall

---

[24] Josemaría Escrivá, *The Way* (New York: Scepter Publishers, 2010), 179.

not offer anything that has a blemish, for it will not be acceptable for you" (Lev 22:20). The ancient Israelites had to offer a perfect lamb as a sacrifice. Likewise, in our sacrifices and throughout the whole of our lives, we want to offer perfect work to God, performing our duties with love, attention to detail, and professional excellence.

The final essential element of priestly character is the apostolate, the spreading of the Gospel. This is as simple as telling other people about our relationship with Jesus and the difference he makes in our lives.

Recovering a robust vision of the common priesthood is essential for answering Protestant objections and Catholic dissentions. We should all be so busy trying to fulfill our callings that we wouldn't need to be ordained to feel important to the mission of God! While we need many men to respond to the call to the priesthood, young men shouldn't respond to this call because they think that's the only way to become significant in salvation history.

To Protestants, Catholicism often looks so passive because so much of the Catholic *laity* is passive. If Catholics understood their priestly calling and were busy fulfilling it in the workplaces and at home, sanctifying their work and offering it to God, and participating in the salvation of the world, then the lure of Protestant activism would not be so attractive.

## Ministerial Priesthood

The second mode of participation in Christ's priesthood is the ministerial priest.

Non-Catholic Christians would agree with a lot of what we just said about the common priesthood; however, they might argue that there is no role for a *ministerial priesthood* anymore in the New Covenant. There is no need for an order of believers dedicated to public worship, no need for office-holders who exercise sacred authority within the body, no need for men who offer sacrifice and mediate the forgiveness of sins. But is that what the New Testament teaches? Did Jesus come to *abolish* the ministerial priesthood or *transform* it?

Let's begin with this concept: the Apostles held an *office*. At the end of the Gospels, we see that the Apostles were commissioned by Jesus to "do" (i.e., "perform") the liturgical sacrifice, Jesus' own memorial offering. This role wasn't given to every single follower of Jesus. The Apostles alone were commissioned to perform that act that we now call a "sacrament." Moreover, this commission of Jesus to the Apostles to perform the Eucharistic sacrifice was not a personal privilege that stopped when those individual Apostles died. Instead, the Apostles fulfilled a role that continues in the Church beyond their personal lifetimes. We can see this in Acts 1 in the account of the replacement of Judas by Matthias:

> In those days Peter stood up among the brethren
> (the company of persons was in all about a hundred
> and twenty) and said, "Brethren, the Scripture had
> to be fulfilled, which the Holy Spirit spoke be-
> forehand by the mouth of David, concerning Judas
> who was guide to those who arrested Jesus. . . . For
> it is written in the book of Psalms, 'Let his habi-
> tation become desolate, and let there be no one to
> live in it'; and 'His *office* let another take.'" (Acts
> 1:15–20, emphasis mine)

Let's examine that last line more closely. In Greek, the
word translated "office" is *episcopē*, literally "bishopric" or
"episcopate." In fact, the King James Bible—rightly be-
loved by many traditional Protestants—translates this line
as "His *bishopric* let another take." The King James translation helps us feel the whole impact of this event, this replacing of one Apostle by another after his death, because
this is really the beginning of what we call *apostolic succession*, which is the continuation of the apostolic ministry
by other men after the death of the Apostles themselves.
The passage from Acts continues:

> "So one of the men who have accompanied us
> during all the time that the Lord Jesus went in
> and out among us, beginning from the baptism
> of John until the day when he was taken up from

us—one of these must become with us a witness to his resurrection." And they put forward two, Joseph called Barsabbas, who was surnamed Justus, and Matthias. And they prayed and said, "Lord, you know the hearts of all men, show which one of these two you have chosen to take the place in this ministry and apostleship from which Judas turned aside, to go to his own place." And they cast lots for them, and the lot fell on Matthias; and he was enrolled with the eleven Apostles. (Acts 1:21–26)

Indeed, as we continue reading in Acts, we see that managing the Church becomes a bigger job than the Apostles can handle by themselves, and so they start to authorize other men to help them. They give other men a role in this office that they themselves had received:

Now in these days when the disciples were increasing in number, the Hellenists murmured against the Hebrews because their widows were neglected in the daily distribution. And the Twelve summoned the body of the disciples and said, "It is not right that we should give up preaching the word of God to serve tables. Therefore, brethren, pick out from among you seven men of good repute, full of the Spirit and of wisdom, whom we may appoint to this duty. But we will devote ourselves to prayer and to the ministry of the word." And what they said pleased the whole multitude, and they chose Stephen, a man full of faith and of the Holy Spirit, and Philip, and Prochorus, and Nicanor, and Timon, and Parmenas, and Nicolaus, a proselyte of Antioch. These they set before the apostles, and they prayed and laid their hands upon them. (Acts 6:1–6)

There are two key points to examine here. First, the Apostles said that they would "appoint to this duty" the men who would help them. These men are not being *elected*; rather, they are being *appointed*. Some readers miss this key point due to the fact that the Apostles allow the laity to propose the men who will be invested with authority. But note well that these men have no authority *until the Apostles lay their hands on them.*

This laying on of hands is the second key point. Here, we find the beginnings of *ordination*, which even today involves the bishop *laying his hands* on the candidate for priesthood. We see this practice of the laying on of hands to transmit the authority that the Apostles had received from Christ also reflected in St. Paul's Epistles to Timothy and Titus. We call these the "Pastoral Epistles" because Timothy and Titus were the equivalent of bishops at this point in time, and have "pastoral" (lit. "shepherding") responsibility over a "flock" (a congregation or community of believers).

St. Paul says to Timothy, "Do not neglect the gift you have, which was given you by prophetic utterance when the presbyters laid their hands upon you" (1 Tim 4:14, translation mine). "Presbyters" is *presbuteroi* in Greek. Its literal meaning is "elders," and it is the word that eventually evolves into the English noun "priest." In this verse, St. Paul is referring to Timothy's ordination, when the presbyters "laid their hands" on Timothy. He also warns Timothy, "Do not be hasty in the laying on of hands, nor participate in another man's sins; keep yourself pure" (1 Tim 5:22). In other words, St. Paul is telling Timothy to be careful whom he ordains. He shouldn't authorize just anyone to celebrate the Eucharist and govern the community because—if they turn out to be spiritually immature—Timothy will have then compounded the problem by putting this person in a place of authority.

Later, St. Paul again says, "For this reason I remind you to rekindle the gift of God that is within you through the laying on of my hands" (2 Tim 1:6). Here, he is referring to his own participation in Timothy's ordination and the charism that Timothy received by what we would now call *Holy Orders*. Likewise, to Titus, St. Paul gives this instruction: "This is why I left you in Crete, that you might amend what was defective, and *appoint presbyters* in every town as I directed you" (Titus 1:5, emphasis and translation mine). Let us observe how the apostolic delegate, Titus, represents

St. Paul by exercising in Crete the kind of authority we now associate with a bishop. Titus has been given the authority to appoint the presbyters, that is, the priests. In passages like these, we can clearly see *apostolic succession*—the continuation of the apostolic ministry by other men—and the sacrament of *Holy Orders* developing.

St. Peter also makes an important contribution to understanding apostolic succession in his first epistle. Peter stresses that the presbyters share in the apostolic ministry to shepherd (pastor) the people of God (1 Pet 5:5). Peter emphasizes the close connection between the presbyters and the Apostles by identifying himself—the chief Apostle—as a presbyter:

> So I exhort the presbyters among you, as a fellow presbyter and a witness of the sufferings of Christ as well as a partaker in the glory that is to be revealed. Tend the flock of God that is your charge. (1 Pet 5:1, translation mine)

This passage needs also to be read against the triple commissioning of Peter as the chief "shepherd" or "pastor" of Jesus' flock in John 21. We see that Peter regards the presbyters as sharing with him his responsibility to shepherd or pastor the people of God. In time, the Church would use the term "successor" and speak of the "successors" of the Apostles.

Let's synthesize what we've discussed up to this point. Jesus appointed leaders, that is, the Apostles, with a priestly duty to "do this in remembrance of me" or "do this as my memorial sacrifice." He also instructs them to baptize, as we read in Matthew, "Go therefore and make disciples of all nations, *baptizing* them in the name of the Father and of the Son and of the Holy Spirit" (Matt 28:19, emphasis mine). So Jesus has appointed the Apostles with a priestly duty to perform the sacraments, *Baptism* and the *Eucharist*.

When the Church became too large for the Apostles alone to govern, as we see in Acts, the Apostles laid their hands on other men to help them fulfill their commission. The men appointed in Acts 6 are traditionally known as the first *diakonoi*, or "deacons" in English. In the rest of Acts and also in the Epistles, we encounter associates of the Apostles called *episkopoi*[25] or bishops, and *presbuteroi* or priests, who *extend* the Apostles' mission beyond their physical presence and *continue it* after their death.[26] This *apostolic succession* continues to this day.

There is no other biblical model of Church government except this top-down system of appointment from the Apostles. One of the big topics within the Protestant tradition of my youth (Calvinism) was, what is the biblical

---

[25] Literally "overseers" and related to *episcopê*, "office of oversight."
[26] Acts 14:23; 15:2–6; 16:4; 20:17, 28; 21:18 Phil 1:1; 1 Tim 3:1–2; 5:17, 19; Titus 1:5, 7; James 5:14; 1 Pet 5:1.

Church government? We would argue constantly about how things really should be run "according to New Testament," about how the Church should be structured "by Scripture." The answer is so obvious in hindsight! This is the biblical model of Church government: the Apostles appointed men by the laying on of hands and they laid hands on others down to the present day. We should obey the men with the hands laid on them.

I've asked some of my Protestant pastor friends what they thought the biblical model of Church government was. Most of them were honest and replied that they didn't know. I've pointed out the passages we discussed above and bring up the laying on of hands and apostolic succession, and gotten this reply: "I can see how you could argue that." Indeed! That's what the mainstream of the Church has always believed.

The men who have received special authority in a chain coming down from the Apostles themselves constitute what we call the *ministerial priesthood*. They have priestly authority and responsibility to do things that the Old Testament priests *used* to do, such as (1) perform sacrifices, (2) forgive sins, and (3) interpret God's law. In the New Covenant, the priestly role of offering sacrifice is bestowed on the Apostles in Luke 22:19 and its parallels ("do this as my memorial sacrifice"). The priestly role of mediating forgiveness is given to the Apostles in John

20:22–23 ("whose sins you forgive are forgiven them"). The priestly role of interpreting the law is given in Matthew 16:19 and 18:18. The Apostles, in turn, share them with men called *episkopoi* and *presbuteroi,* "bishops" and "priests," as we see in Acts and the Epistles.

These men continue to fulfill the roles of the Old Testament ministerial priesthood, and this is their unique participation in Christ's priesthood. The rest of us don't perform those specific roles. We don't offer the sacraments. Without any guidance or governing structure, we would quickly realize how miserable a situation like that really is, and—more importantly—that it is not the system we see established by Jesus and the Apostles in the pages of the New Testament. St. Paul exhorts us to "Obey your leaders and submit to them, for they are keeping watch over your souls, as those who will have to give account. Let them do this with joy, and not sadly, for that would be of no advantage to you" (Heb 13:17).

Notice that this little passage simply presumes that there *were* already appointed "leaders" in all the Christian communities to which this apostolic epistle would reach, and furthermore that the leadership was particularly spiritual in nature ("keeping watch over *your souls*"!) and constituted a sacred trust for which they would answer to God Himself ("those who will have to *give an account*"; cf. Luke 16:2; Rom 14:12). We don't have a picture of each congregation electing and deposing whomever they will as their ecclesiastical "representatives."

When read carefully, we observe in the Lord's ministry as recorded in the Gospels, as well as in the history of the early Church as recorded in Acts and reflected in the Epistles, that roles and responsibilities once exercised by the Aaronic priesthood with the support of the Levites were quite consciously handed over by Christ to the Apostles, and then shared by the Apostles with other men whom they designated as *presbuteroi* (priests) and *episkopoi* (bishops). Striking confirmation of his understanding of the text of Scripture as well as the historical origin of the Church's hierarchy can be found in the First Epistle of Clement to the Corinthians (*1 Clement*), in which Clement, the *episkopos* of Rome, writes to the church in Corinth specifically to correct a certain "democratic" view of Church office that the congregation there held, such that the laity felt free to depose duly appointed *presbyters*. Clement writes:

> Our apostles likewise knew, through our Lord Jesus Christ, that there would be strife over the bishop's office. For this reason, therefore, having received complete foreknowledge, they appointed the officials mentioned earlier and afterwards they gave the offices a permanent character; that is, if they should die, other approved men should

succeed to their ministry. Those, therefore, who were appointed by them or, later on, by other reputable men with the consent of the whole Church, and who have ministered to the flock of Christ blamelessly, humbly, peaceably, and unselfishly, and for a long time have been well-spoken of by all—these men we consider to be unjustly removed from their ministry. For it will be no small sin for us, if we depose from the bishop's office those who have offered the gifts blamelessly and in holiness. Blessed are those presbyters who have gone on ahead, who took their departure at a mature and fruitful age, for they need no longer fear that someone might remove them from their established place. (1 Clem 44:1–5)

Equally striking, however, is an earlier passage in which Clement stressed the continuity between the leadership of the Old Testament people of God and that of the New Testament Church:

Since, therefore, these things are now clear to us and we have searched into the depths of the divine knowledge, we ought to do, in order, everything that the Master has commanded us to perform at the appointed times. Now he commanded the offerings and services to be performed diligently, and not to be done carelessly or in disorder, but at designated times and occasions. Both where and by whom he wants them to be performed, he himself has determined by his supreme will, so that all things, being done devoutly according to his good pleasure, may be acceptable to his will. Those, therefore, who make their offerings at the appointed times are acceptable and blessed, for those who follow the instructions of the Master cannot go wrong. For to the *high priest* the proper services have been given, and to the *priests* the proper office has been assigned, and upon the *Levites* the proper ministries have been imposed. The layman is bound by the layman's rules. Let each of you, brothers, give thanks to God with your own group, maintaining a good conscience, not overstepping the designated rule of his ministry, but acting with reverence. (1 Clem 40:1–41:1)

In verse five above, St. Clement is actually describing the Christian hierarchy, but he calls them by their Old Covenant names: the "bishop" is referred to as "high priest," the presbyters as "priests," the deacons as "Levites," and finally the laity are called by their common name. This provides a clear witness to the fact that this continuity is not something invented retrospectively by clever theologians or Bible scholars, but something that was readily recognized and even somewhat commonplace for the early Christian community.

## Call No Man "Father"

To conclude this chapter, let's discuss the idea of calling priests "father." In Matthew 23:9, when Jesus says, "And call no man your father on earth, for you have one Father, who is in heaven," does Jesus mean that literally or is he just driving home a point using strong terminology? I would say it's the latter. Catholics are criticized for this because Catholics call priests "father."

When Jesus said to "call no man your father on earth, for you have one Father, who is in heaven," he is using an expression that has deep roots in the Hebrew Scriptures. To "call" someone by a "name" in the Hebrew tradition meant something closer to "identifying the essence" of a person. For example, when the prophet Isaiah says of the Messiah that "his name will be called Wonderful Counselor, the Mighty God, Everlasting Father, Prince of Peace," he certainly does *not* mean that those titles will be commonly used as names of the Messiah by his contemporaries. None of Jesus' contemporaries, not even the Apostles themselves, called him those things. Rather, the "name" here means the *essence*, and Isaiah is describing the *nature* of the Messiah, who will be, in his very nature, the "Mighty God" who shares the essence of the "Wonderful

Counselor" (the Holy Spirit) and the "Everlasting Father" (God the Father).

So, in this Hebrew tradition, when Jesus says, "Call no one on earth your father," he means, "Recognize no one on earth as your father in his *essence* for by nature and by essence, there is only one Father, that is, God the Father." In a very real sense, all other fathers, even one's own biological father, are *imitation* fathers, because God is the true Father who begets children in a way that only He, as God, can. When you were conceived, God created your soul *de novo*, "new," and *ex nihilo*, "from nothing." That is true fatherhood!

Your biological father did not create anything *de novo* or *ex nihilo*. Your biological father contributed to your body in a physical process that was wondrously fashioned by God, but nonetheless completely *natural* and according to physical laws. In a very real sense, your physical father is only a father by analogy, that is, human fatherhood is *similar* to true fatherhood, which God alone exercises. Another way to look at it is that we can call our biological fathers "Father" only because God is our true Father. All paternity is an imitation of the paternity of God the Father, as St. Paul says: "I bow my knees before the Father, from whom all fatherhood [Greek *patria*] in heaven and on earth is named" (Eph 3:14–15, my translation).

Likewise, ministerial priests are like God the Father, who begets in a spiritual and supernatural way. As some theologians have pointed out, the ministerial priest is *more* like God the Father than a biological father is. When a ministerial priest baptizes a baby, he's bringing about new spiritual life. Through the Word and the Spirit he is "birthing" a soul, moving it from death into life. This is more like how God creates a soul than like biological procreation. True fatherhood is spiritual in its essence. So, when Jesus says, "call no man your father on earth, for you have one Father, who is in heaven," he is emphasizing that all true paternity is in God the Father, and all human paternity is only an imitation of divine paternity.

Nonetheless, both Jesus and the Apostles continue to call men "fathers" in their teaching and conversation. In Luke 16:24, for example, Jesus tells a parable in which he refers to Israel's great ancestor as *"Father* Abraham." Likewise, St. Paul, in his Letter to the Romans, refers to Abraham as the *"father* of all . . . who believe" (Rom 4:11). A few verses later, St. Paul again calls Abraham the *"father* of us all" (Rom 4:16). In his Letter to the Philippians, St. Paul says that Timothy, "as a son with a *father* . . . has served with me in the gospel" (Phil 2:22). In his First Letter to the Corinthians, St. Paul says, "For I became your *father* in Christ Jesus through the gospel" (1 Cor 4:15). This is particularly significant because he is claiming a spiritual role of fatherhood for himself. Later, he says, "I want you to know, brethren, that our *fathers* were all under the cloud, and all passed through the sea" (1 Cor 10:1). In Galatians, he talks about how he was "extremely zealous . . . for the traditions of my *fathers*" (Gal 1:14). In Thessalonians, he describes himself as "like a *father*" (1 Thess 2:11). In 1 Timothy, he instructs Timothy to "not rebuke an older man but exhort him as you would a *father*" (1 Tim 5:1). In Philemon, he says, "I appeal to you for my child, Onesimus, whose *father* I have become in my imprisonment" (Phlm 1:10), here again, identifying himself a spiritual father.

The most interesting, perhaps, of all these examples, is in 1 John, where the Apostle says: "I am writing to you, fathers, because you know him who is from the beginning. I am writing to you, young men, because you have overcome the Evil One. I write to you, children, because you know the Father" (1 John 2:13–14).

Now, most commentators, going all the way back to the Church Fathers, don't think that St. John is speaking to woodenly literal groups here, as if "fathers" means all those and only those men in the congregation who have biological children, and "young men" means all the males of the congregation between fifteen and twenty-five, and "children" refers to the youngsters up to age fourteen. No, the context begs for these terms to be understood as categories of spiritual maturity and/or role in the church community. Even Protestant commentators will acknowledge that "fathers" probably corresponds to the presbyters or "elders" (Greek *presbuteroi*) of the congregation; the "young men" refer to those Christians who had completed initiation, that is, who had completed basic catechesis and were growing deeper in their faith; and "children" were recent converts receiving formation or in other words, the catechumens. The first person recorded as addressing Christian presbyters (priests) as "fathers" turns out to be one of chief Apostles, and he does so in the very pages of the Scriptures themselves.

## SUMMARY

We've looked at the abundance of priestly themes in the New Testament. Examining more closely the presentation of Jesus in the Temple (Luke 2:22–24), we saw that the intention of his parents may have been to present Jesus to God as a "priest forever." Mary and Joseph did not offer to "redeem" Jesus or "buy him back" from the obligations of his priestly role as the firstborn male child, which had become the Jewish practice after the priesthood was transferred to the Levites as God's response to His people worshiping the golden calf.

We pointed to Jesus claiming a priestly privilege and establishing a new priesthood for both himself and his Apostles (Matt 12:1–8). This new priesthood is based not on that of Levi but like that of Melchizedek (cf. Ps 110:4), who was a "perpetual" priest.

We saw that when Jesus speaks of his body as the new temple (John 2:18–22), he is also identifying himself as the new high priest, the new Adam, whose body represents and concentrates, so to speak, the cosmic temple. Jesus' Apostles participated in his new priesthood and exercised priestly duties to perform the sacraments (1 Cor 11:23–24). The men who received authority in a long line of succession from the Apostles make up the ministerial priesthood (Luke 22:19; John 20:22–23; Matt 16:19 and 18:18) and participate uniquely in Christ's priesthood.

We observed that the Scriptures record the Apostles giving other men a role in their priestly office that they themselves had received (Acts 1:15–20; 6:1–6). These men were not *elected* but were *appointed*. The New Testament practice of laying hands on chosen individuals to transmit the authority that the Apostles had received from Christ, reflected in St. Paul's Epistles to Timothy (1 Tim 4:14; 5:22; 2 Tim 1:6), is the original form of *ordination* that continues in practice today, with each new priest receiving the hands of his bishop. Thus, the New Testament clearly shows an *apostolic succession*—the continuation of the apostolic ministry by other men—and the sacrament of *Holy Orders* developing (1 Tim 4:14; 5:22; 2 Tim 1:6; Titus 1:5; 1 Pet 5:1).

We also looked at the concept of the common priesthood that is reflected in several important places in the New Testament (e.g., Rom 12:1), where we are encouraged to offer our bodies and our entire lives as living sacrifices. We are to express our common priesthood primarily not in the liturgy but in the world, through living an ordinary life with extraordinary holiness. The essential elements of a priestly character are made up of prayer, mortification, excellence in our work, and spreading the Gospel.

We concluded this chapter by examining Jesus' apparent prohibition against calling anyone "father" (Matt 23:9). The expression that Jesus was using must be understood against the backdrop of the Scriptures and Hebrew thought: to "call" someone by a "name" in the Hebrew tradition meant something closer to "identifying the essence" of a person. We asserted that the admonition to "call no one on earth your father" means more specifically to recognize no one on earth as your father *in his essence*. In essence, there is only one true Father: God the Father. Other evidence in the New Testament writings supports this interpretation, as both Jesus and the Apostles continue to call men "father" in their teaching and conversation (Luke 16:24, Rom 4:11, 16; Phil 2:22; 1 Cor 4:15; 10:1; Gal 1:14; 1 Thess 2:11; 1 Tim 5:1; Phlm 1:10).

## QUESTIONS

1. In what ways does Jesus' presentation in the temple point to the priesthood?

2. What are the similarities between Jesus and Samuel?

3. Explain the concept of "binding and loosing"—particularly how it was understood in the Old Testament. Why does it point to a new priesthood in the New Covenant?

4. Describe how Jesus washed the feet of his disciples and why his words and actions relate to the priesthood.

5. What is the culmination of the consecration of the Apostles as priests? At that time, what priestly role is given to them?

6. What is the "blood of the covenant"? Where is this phrase used in the Old Testament?

7. According to first-century Jews, what kind of priest was Jesus?

8. What is the difference between the ministerial priesthood and the common priesthood? What are the similarities?

9. Did Jesus come to *abolish* the ministerial priesthood or *transform* it? Provide evidence.

10. Give two examples from the New Testament that reflect priesthood concepts.

CHAPTER 4

# THE SCROLLS, CELIBACY, AND HOLY ORDERS

Growing up as a Protestant, I had a very dim view of priestly celibacy. No one practices celibacy in Protestantism despite the fact that Jesus recommends it (Matt 19:12) as does St. Paul (1 Cor 7:32–35). The arguments challenging priestly celibacy go like this: celibacy is unbiblical; Jewish men all married, and so Jesus was married (Dan Brown, *The Da Vinci Code*); Jesus' followers were all equal. Bishops, priests, and deacons are a late corruption; celibacy was imposed by the pope in the Middle Ages in order to acquire the property of clergymen; the Catholic Church got its "negative" views of sexuality from St. Augustine.

None of that is true, of course. As we'll see, celibacy was a way of life practiced by some of the ancient Israelite prophets, like Elijah, Elisha, and Jeremiah, and it was embraced also by John the Baptist, John the Apostle, St.

Paul, and Our Lord himself. It's stunning that some will criticize as "unbiblical" or "unnatural" the very lifestyle Jesus himself chose to live for our salvation!

Let's take a look at both celibacy and Holy Orders in the Dead Sea Scrolls, the Scriptures, and the Church. My research on the Dead Sea Scrolls led me to many interesting discoveries about the practice of celibacy in Judaism at the time of Our Lord. For example, when I was younger, this saying of Jesus always puzzled me:

> He said to them ... "whoever divorces his wife, except for unchastity, and marries another, commits adultery; and he who marries a divorced woman, commits adultery." The disciples said to him, "If such is the case of a man with his wife, it is not expedient to marry." But he said to them, "Not all men can receive this precept, but only those to whom it is given. *For there are eunuchs who have been so from birth, and there are eunuchs who have been made eunuchs by men, and there are eunuchs who have made themselves eunuchs for the sake of the kingdom of heaven.* He who is able to receive this, let him receive it." (Matt 19:8–12, emphasis mine)

I understood well enough that "eunuchs who have been so from birth" must mean men born with a condition such that they cannot have children, and I also knew what "eunuchs who have been made eunuchs by men" meant: it was common practice for kings in the ancient Near East to employ eunuchs to watch over the royal harems and to serve in other offices in the palace, so much so that in some ancient languages the word for "eunuch" and "royal officer" are often the same.[1] But what puzzled me was the phrase "eunuchs who have made themselves eunuchs for the sake of the kingdom of heaven." I knew that had to refer to men who voluntarily accepted celibacy for religious reasons, but who was doing this in Jesus' day? After all, he does not say, "There *will be* men who *will make* themselves eunuchs for the sake of the kingdom," but "there *are* eunuchs who *have made* themselves eunuchs for the sake of the kingdom of heaven." So clearly, Jesus is speaking about celibate men of his own day, who are celibate for "the kingdom of heaven."

But everyone knows, as the argument goes, that Jesus' contemporaries were Jews, not Christians, and Jews do not practice celibacy. A good Jew takes God's blessing to "be fruitful and multiply" (Gen 1:22) as one of the first, if not *the* first, *mitzvah* (commandment) in the *Torah*, and therefore he has a moral obligation to find a wife and raise children for the glory of God and the people of Israel.

In the course of my doctoral work I discovered that

---

[1] For example, in Hebrew, the term *saris* covers both concepts, e.g., Genesis 39:1; Isaiah 56:3–4.

Jesus is speaking of the Jewish sect known as the Essenes, who along with the Pharisees and Sadducees made up the three major schools of thought and religious practice in the time of Our Lord. The Essenes practiced celibacy and founded monasteries where Jewish men lived in community, praying, working, and worshiping while they awaited the coming of the Messiah. The Essenes had a monastery on the shores of the Dead Sea. They hid their library in the caves around their settlement out of fear of Roman attack in the AD 60s, and the remains of that library are what we know as the celebrated Dead Sea Scrolls.

The Essenes regarded themselves as the heirs of both the prophets and the priesthood, and their practice of celibacy was one of the most notable features of their religious lifestyle. All the classical scholars that describe the Essenes—Josephus, Philo, Pliny, along with some less important writers—remark on their celibacy. For example, the Roman scholar Pliny the Elder wrote: "The solitary tribe of the Essenes which is remarkable beyond all the other tribes of the whole world as it has no women and has renounced all sexual desire."[2] Josephus and Pliny wrote:

> These Essenes reject pleasures as an evil, but esteem continence, and the conquest over our passions, to be virtue. They neglect wedlock, but

---

[2] Pliny the Elder, *Pliny—Natural History II*, trans. H. Rackham (Loeb Classical Library, Cambridge: Harvard University Press, 1942), 277.

choose out other persons' children . . . and form them according to their own manners.[3]

They repudiate marriage; and at the same time they practice continence in an eminent degree; for no one of the Essenes ever marries a wife . . .[4]

It is a remarkable convergence that not one but three ancient scholars would record that the Essenes were celibate. Moreover, their testimony to this practice is not limited to an isolated comment, but all three also go on to describe the kind of communal life the Essenes lived, without ever mentioning women or children as being present among them—and indeed, the austere Essene lifestyle the classical authors describe leaves no room at all for raising one's own family. The Essenes lived an ascetical life with meals, possessions, and finances in common—and whether then or now, one cannot raise a family in circumstances like that.

Some scholars have argued that the classical authors were wrong about the Essenes because they were affected by a supposedly "pro-celibacy" worldview of antiquity. But there is no evidence that Josephus, Philo, or Pliny were pro-celibacy. None of them were themselves celibate, and, with one exception, they do not claim in their writings

---

[3] Flavius Josephus , *The Works of Josephus: Complete and Unabridged*, trans. William Whitson (Peabody, MA: Hendrickson, 1987), 605.

[4] Philo, *Hypothetica*, 11:14, in *The Works of Philo: Complete and Unabridged*, trans. C.D. Yonge (Peabody, MA: Hendrickson, 1996), 746.

that any other groups besides the Essenes were celibate.[5] Greco-Roman culture did not encourage or promote celibacy. True, the ancient authors were impressed by the Essenes' self-control, but not so much that they wanted to adopt the lifestyle for themselves!

Other scholars argue that the idea the Essenes were celibate largely arose because certain Catholic priests like Fr. Roland de Vaux played a leading role in the initial discovery of the scrolls and popularized the idea. But many, many scholars of a wide variety of religious and ethnic backgrounds—including Israeli scholars of such eminence as Yigael Yadin, Elisha Qimron, and Magen Broshi—have been convinced the Qumran Essenes were celibate.

Others insist that it is only the external testimony of the classical authors that suggests the Qumran site was inhabited by celibate men. If we went on the basis of the archeological remains and Dead Sea Scrolls themselves, the argument goes, we would never get the idea that the Qumran Essenes were celibate. The problem with this argument is that both the scrolls and the archeology suggest a celibate male community lived at Qumran.

Archeologically, we find almost no feminine-gendered objects at Qumran—things like jewelry, certain kinds of

---

[5] Philo does also describe as celibate another very Essene-like group of Jews known as the *Therapeutae*. But the Therapeutae included women. Outside of Judaism, the only classical group thought to have practiced celibacy was the Pythagoreans.

combs, hand mirrors, or spindles, which are found at other Jewish sites from the period and are reliable indicators of the presence of women. Furthermore, although some female skeletons have been found in the cemetery, further investigation has shown that these burials were probably not from the time period when the Qumran community was occupied. There is not a single undisputed female or child skeleton among the more than thirty skeletons exhumed from the main cemetery, which consists of nearly one thousand north-south oriented shaft graves. We should recall that in most ancient cemeteries, adult men make up less than 25 percent of the remains. Moreover, these graves themselves seem to indicate the rejection of family life, because each one contains but one skeleton, although regular Jewish custom at the time practiced family burials, where all members of a nuclear or even extended family were interred in a common cave or tomb.

Even without the external historical witness, the absence of women and children from the *Community Rule* and their nearly complete absence from the archeological record at Qumran would be more than enough evidence to raise the suspicion that whoever lived here rejected the normal form of Jewish family life.[6]

---

[6] For further discussion and scholarly references on celibacy at Qumran, see my *Jesus and the Dead Sea Scrolls: Revealing the Jewish Roots of Christianity* (New York: Penguin Random House, 2019), 125–139.

## The Old Testament Basis for Celibacy

The obvious question is, why were they practicing celibacy? The theology of celibacy develops in the Old Testament from two sources: (1) Priestly: the cleanliness requirements of the priesthood, and (2) Prophetic: the rigors of the prophetic vocation.

Priestly ritual cleanliness comes from Leviticus 15:18: "If a man lies with a woman . . . both of them shall bathe themselves in water, and be unclean until the evening." And physical relations made one unfit for acts of worship, in contrast to other ancient religions that employed them as part of worship (e.g., Corinth).

Although the Essenes never explicitly provide a rationale in their internal documents, it's pretty straightforward to arrive at the reason: marital relations rendered one unclean, and the Qumranites never wanted to be unclean! They aspired to "perfect holiness"—and cleanliness, while not the same as holiness, was a pre-requisite for holiness.

For example, the famous passage from the Damascus Document reads:

> In short, for all who conduct their lives by these laws, *in perfect holiness*, according to all the instructions, God's covenant stands firm to give them life for thousands of generations. *But* if they live in camps according to the rule of the land and

marry women and beget children, then let them live in accordance with the Law . . .[7]

This passage contrasts two different lifestyles: the life of "perfect holiness" and the life of "living in camps" where they "marry and beget children." The unavoidable implication, then, is that the life of "perfect holiness" means giving up marriage and children. Such persons need some encouragement because they lack the natural consolation of seeing their own offspring carry on their legacy. The Damascus Document provides that encouragement: "God's covenant stands firm to give them life for thousands of generations."

The other group that marries and raises children must certainly be the "other order of Essenes" that Josephus alone mentions—an order of Essenes that lives regular family life:

Moreover, there is another order of Essenes, who agree with the rest as to their way of living, and customs, and laws, but differ from them in the point of marriage, as thinking that by not marrying they cut off the principal part of the human life . . .[8]

---

[7] *Damascus Document*, quoted in John Bergsma, *Jesus and the Dead Sea Scrolls: Revealing the Jewish Roots of Christianity* (New York: Penguin Random House, 2019), 8.

[8] Josephus, *The Works of Josephus: Complete and Unabridged*, 607.

What percentage of the Essene movement belonged to the marrying branch is an open question. From the fact that the ancient authors describe the celibate Essenes almost exclusively, it would seem that the marrying Essenes were not characteristic of the movement as a whole. The majority of the movement was attracted to the idea of "perfect holiness," a concept I would argue does not mean celibacy *per se*, but a lifestyle in which one never becomes unclean—at least not voluntarily—and thus would *include* celibacy while not *defined* by celibacy.

Interwoven with their desire to live "perfect holiness" was the Qumranites' self-conception as a priesthood and a temple. Referring to the *Yahad* of Qumran, the *Community Rule* states:

> They will be "the tested wall, the precious cornerstone" (Isaiah 28:16) whose foundations shall neither be shaken nor swayed, a fortress, a *Holy of Holies for Aaron*, all of them knowing the Covenant of Justice and thereby offering a sweet savor. They shall be *a blameless and true House* in Israel, upholding the covenant of eternal statutes. (*The Community Rule* [1QS] 8:7–10)[9]

"House of God" is the Hebrew idiom for a temple, and the description "*blameless and true House*" is temple language.

---

[9]   Quoted in Bergsma, *Jesus and the Dead Sea Scrolls*, 173–174.

The Qumran community regarded themselves as the dwelling place of the Spirit of God, not merely a temple but truly a "Holy of Holies for Aaron," that is, the most holy part of the Temple where atonement could be made for all the people. The Holy of Holies is where national atonement was performed on *Yom Kippur*, the holiest day of the Jewish liturgical year.

However, nothing unclean could enter the Temple, and it was unthinkable that anyone would engage in marital relations in the Temple because such an act rendered the persons and their environment unclean. Therefore, the Essenes forbade not only relations in the Temple but indeed in the entire city of Jerusalem:

> No m[an] who has a nocturnal emission is to enter any part of My temple until three [com]plete days have passed. He must launder his clothes and bathe on the first day; on the third he must again launder and bathe; then, after the sun has set, he may enter the temple. They are not to enter My temple while unclean, for that would defile it. If a man has intercourse with his wife, he may not enter any part of the temple city (where I shall make My name to dwell) for three days. (*The Temple Scroll* [11QTemple[a]] 45:7–12)[10]

---

[10] Quoted in Bergsma, *Jesus and the Dead Sea Scrolls*, 134.

But since the Qumran community regarded themselves as not only a substitute Temple but a "Holy of Holies for Aaron," it followed that every member of the community had to live the life of "perfect holiness," never *willfully* engaging in any activity that rendered them unclean, including intercourse. It's not clear whether the Qumran community defined the extent of their human "temple" by geography—up to the border of their settlement, for example—or by membership, such that the "temple" extended to each person who had entered the covenant of their community. But for daily life at Qumran, the distinction would have been insignificant: intercourse and other defiling actions could not take place within the community, period.

The early Church, like the Qumran *Yahad*, regarded itself as a human temple. Paul's Letter to the Ephesians impresses on young Christians:

> You are fellow citizens with the saints and members of the household of God, built upon the foundation of the apostles and prophets, Christ Jesus himself being the cornerstone, in whom the whole structure is joined together and grows into a holy temple in the Lord. (Eph 2:19–21)

The temple was not geographical, but extended to every member of the Church. Elsewhere Paul reminds the first Christians: "Do you not know that your body is a temple of the Holy Spirit within you, which you have from God?" (1 Cor 6:19).

## UNDIVIDED DEVOTION TO THE LORD

Interestingly, the early Church, like Qumran, saw a direct link between the temple nature of the community and sexual behavior. Because they are the temple of the Holy Spirit, Paul emphatically warns Christians:

> Do you not know that your bodies are members of Christ? Shall I therefore take the members of Christ and make them members of a prostitute? Never! . . . Shun [sexual] immorality [*porneia*, in the Greek]. Every other sin which a man commits is outside the body; but the immoral man sins against his own body. (1 Cor 6:15, 18)

While the Qumranites required abstention from all intercourse for their temple-members, the Church required abstention only outside of marriage. Intercourse of husband and wife was considered pure in itself: "Let marriage be held in honor among all, and let the marriage bed be undefiled; for God will judge the immoral and adulterous" (Heb 13:4).

That is not to say that early Christians did not place value on celibacy. Like the Essenes, and unlike the Pharisees and Sadducees, the young Church had great respect for the celibate state, although for different reasons. For the Essenes, as we've seen, celibacy was part of the larger effort to live a life of perfect ritual cleanliness. For Christians, the issue was not ritual cleanliness but a freedom from the obligations of family life in order to be wholly dedicated to the Lord. This is reflected in Jesus' own teaching: "There are eunuchs who have made themselves eunuchs for the sake of the kingdom of heaven. He who is able to receive this, let him receive it" (Matt 19:12), meaning celibacy for a spiritual goal was a noble state and those that were able to live it should. St. Paul, too, in his long discussion of marriage in his Letters to Corinth, emphasizes the value of celibacy, which he himself practiced:

> It is well for a man not to touch a woman. . . . I wish that all were as I myself am. But each has his own special gift from God, one of one kind and one of another. To the unmarried and the widows I say that it is well for them to remain single as I do. But if they cannot exercise self-control, they should marry. . . . Yet those who marry will have worldly troubles, and I would spare you that. . . . I want you to be free from anxieties. The unmarried man is anxious about the affairs of the Lord, how to please the Lord; but the married man is anxious about worldly affairs, how to please his wife, and his interests are divided. . . . I say this for your own

benefit, not to lay any restraint upon you, but to promote good order and to secure your undivided devotion to the Lord. (1 Cor 7:1, 7–9, 28, 32–35)

The point, then, of Christian celibacy, is not ritual cleanliness but "undivided devotion to the Lord." But we shouldn't draw the contrast between Essenes and Christians too starkly, because in Essenism the concern for ritual cleanliness was not for its own sake, but rather for the sake of always being able to worship, which uncleanness prevented. So for the Essenes, too, celibacy was *ultimately* for the sake of "undivided devotion" to the Lord God of Israel.

In the early Church, this undivided devotion was expected especially of clergy, and some early Church councils record that celibacy for the leaders of the Church was a tradition going back to the Apostles:

It is fitting that the holy bishops and priests of God as well as the Levites [=deacons], that is, those who are in the service of the divine sacraments, observe perfect continence, so that they may obtain in all simplicity what they are asking from God; *what the Apostles taught and what antiquity itself observed*, let us also endeavor to keep. . . . It pleases us all that bishop, priest, and deacon, guardians of purity, abstain from [conjugal intercourse] with their wives, so that those who serve at the altar may keep a perfect chastity. (Council of Carthage, AD 390)[11]


## Priestly Continence

For the priests, too, there was a kind of periodic celibacy. According to the Law of Moses, marital relations rendered one unclean for at least a day (Lev 15:18), and so a priest on continuous duty in the sanctuary could not engage in relations with his wife (Lev 22:1–6). Priests thus had to remain "celibate" for stretches of time when they were on duty at the Temple, and the opportunity to conceive a child was limited to those times when they were "off duty," so to speak—that is, they had a stretch of days when they were not required to serve.

The early Church practiced continence for clergy, but this was not necessarily opposed to marriage. Rather, clergy were expected to keep continent after receiving Holy Orders, even if they were married. In some parts of the Church this rule was not well kept, leading to scandal. Siricius, a bishop of Rome during the lifetime of St. Augustine, remarks in one of his letters, "We have indeed discovered that many priests and deacons of Christ brought

---

[11] This is a quote by Bishop Genethlius, which was ratified by the members of the council. See Christian Cochini, S.J., *Apostolic Origins of Priestly Celibacy*, trans. Nelly Marans (San Francisco: Ignatius, 1990), 5, emphasis mine.

children into the world, either through union with their wives or through shameful intercourse."[12] Despite that, influential Church Fathers, such as St. Augustine, St. Ambrose, St. Jerome, and St. Hilary, were convinced that only the celibate life was compatible with the total dedication that the pastor should have to the Lord and his Bride, the Church. This conviction won the day in the Latin-speaking Church, such that by the time of Pope Leo the Great (400–461), celibacy was the dominant lifestyle of clergy in the West.

Throughout the history of Christianity there have been many Christians inspired by the lifestyle of Jesus, the Apostles Paul and John, and many others to embrace the undivided devotion to the Lord that a life of singleness affords. These believers were called the "single ones,"—in Greek, "single" is *monos*, which was borrowed into Latin as *monachos*. In time, the single Christians gathered into communities called *monasteria*, where they would work, pray, and worship together—unwittingly recreating the communal life the Essenes at Qumran used to live. In English, the single male Christians became known as "monks" and their dwellings "monasteries." And when, centuries later, the dwelling and the writings of Qumran were rediscovered, Western scholars immediately recognized the deep similarities of lifestyle and referred to the

---

[12] Cochini, S.J., *Apostolic Origins of Priestly Celibacy*, 9.

ancient Qumranites as "Jewish monks."

## THE TRADITION OF PROPHETIC CELIBACY

Celibacy was rooted in concepts of prophethood and priesthood. Sometimes a prophet remained single as a sign that "now" was not the time to raise a family, because God was bringing an awful punishment on the people. And so celibacy was a sign of impending judgment on the contemporary age: "The word of the Lord came to me: 'You shall not take a wife, nor shall you have sons or daughters in this place.' For thus says the Lord concerning the sons and daughters who are born in this place. . . . They shall die of deadly diseases. They shall not be lamented, nor shall they be buried" (Jer 16:1–4).

There was also the practical reason that the demanding lifestyle of a prophet was incompatible with both the responsibilities and pleasures of family life. So there was a certain tradition of prophetic celibacy. Prophetic figures who were celibate include Elijah and Elisha, who gave up regular family life in order to serve their divine calling. God commanded Jeremiah to remain single as a witness to his contemporaries (Jer 16:1–4). Ezekiel was a widower for the same reason (Ezek 24:15–24). As mentioned earlier, St. John the Baptist, Our Lord himself, St. John the Evangelist, St. Paul, and others were celibate.

## Rabbi-Synagogue and Priest-Temple

The idea that ancient Israelites were opposed to celibacy is an anachronism—an idea that doesn't fit into its time period. Although modern Rabbinic Judaism strongly encourages every Jewish man to raise children, the same compulsion was not felt in ancient times. As we've shown, celibacy was practiced by the ancient Israelite prophets.

One day during my doctoral seminar, my Judaism professor, herself the daughter of a rabbi, admonished me to be careful to distinguish Judaism from the religion of ancient Israel. The religious system that we call Judaism, or, more accurately, Rabbinic Judaism, is largely a post-biblical development, that is to say, it developed after the books that make up the Old Testament (the Hebrew Bible) had been written. And there are dramatic differences between the way ancient Israelites practiced their religion and modern Jews practice theirs.

For example, the religion of the devout ancient Israelite—as reflected in the Bible—revolved around the Temple and the priesthood. There were three major annual feasts for which the Israelite would go on pilgrimage up to the Temple to offer animals in sacrifice, with the assistance of the priests. In addition, when the Israelite committed a grave sin—or conversely, experienced a great blessing—he would travel to the Temple to offer an animal in sacrifice either for atonement or thanksgiving, respectively. Temple, priesthood, sacrifice—these were central to the ancient Israelite.

By contrast, the life of the modern Jew revolves around the synagogue, the rabbi, the study of Torah, and prayer. The Old Testament does not mention synagogues or rabbis. A synagogue is not a temple. It is not even primarily a place of worship. The term "synagogue" is Greek for "coming together," and synagogues developed in the Hellenistic period (c. 300–100 BC) when Jews were scattered around the Mediterranean too far to travel to the Temple. So to maintain their faith they established common houses to gather together for prayer and to study the Scriptures. The teachers of the Scriptures became known as "rabbis," and so the tradition began and continues to this day.

In the lifetime of Jesus, both systems—the rabbi-synagogue and the priest-Temple—were operational in the land of Israel. Jews in the land of Israel prayed weekly or daily in the synagogue, but then also made pilgrimage to offer animal sacrifice in the Temple according to the law of Moses. In AD 70 the Romans destroyed the Temple in Jerusalem. The priesthood was dispersed and it left only the rabbi-synagogue system, which developed further in order to adapt the law of Moses for observance because its central focus—the sanctuary or Temple—was no longer in existence. The body of law that developed from this process was collected in various documents, like the *Mishnah* (c. AD 200) and the *Talmud* (c. AD 600).

## SUMMARY

We began this chapter by raising common objections to priestly celibacy: that it's unbiblical, that all ancient Jewish men married, that celibacy was imposed by the pope in the Middle Ages to acquire priests' property, that the Catholic Church harbors "negative" views of sexuality because of St. Augustine, and more.

We demonstrated through the Scriptures and the Dead Sea Scrolls that both celibacy and an early form or proto-type of Holy Orders were present in ancient Jewish practice and at the inception of Christianity. We saw this in the figures of Elijah, Elisha, Jeremiah, John the Baptist, John the Apostle, Paul, and Jesus, all celibate men. We pointed out that Jesus spoke specifically of celibate men for "the kingdom of heaven" (Matt 19:8–12) and recommended it (Matt 19:12), as did Paul (1 Cor 7:32–35).

We further corroborated the existence of celibacy in Jesus' time in the Jewish sect of the Essenes, who practiced celibacy and founded monasteries where Jewish men lived in community. The scrolls and ancillary archeological finds at Qumran on the shores of the Dead Sea reveal that the Essenes embraced the lifestyle and saw themselves as the heirs of the Israelite prophethood and the priesthood.

We observed that biblical celibacy arises from these two sources: the priestly (for ritual cleanliness) and the prophetic (as eschatological sign, and for the rigors of the prophetic vocation). We examined the concept of priestly ritual cleanliness in Leviticus 15:18, which stipulates that marital relations rendered one as unclean, and we saw the influence of this concept in the Essenes' aspirations to "perfect holiness" and therefore to be always "clean," which led them to embrace a celibate lifestyle, even if they were not *defined* by celibacy.

We found that the concept and practice of celibacy continued in the early Church (Eph 2:19–21; 1 Cor 6:19) and we pointed out the similarities between the early Church and the Essenes: both believed there was a link between the temple nature of the community and sexual behavior (1 Cor 6:15, 18), although the rationale differed. Ritual cleanliness motivated the Essenes, while "undivided devotion to the Lord"—free from the obligations to raise a family—inspired the Church. Such influential Church Fathers as Augustine, Ambrose, Jerome, and Hilary strongly supported the celibate life, and celibacy became the dominant lifestyle of clergy in the West by the fifth century. The Council of Carthage in AD 390 asserted that celibacy for the leaders of the Church was a tradition going back to the Apostles.

We recognized a form of periodic celibacy for married

priests in ancient Israel when on duty in the sanctuary (Lev 22:1–6), and we saw the early Church take this a step further by practicing continence for clergy after receiving Holy Orders—even if they were married.

Lastly, we compared the way a largely post-biblical Rabbinic Judaism practice their faith—comprised of the synagogue, the rabbi, and the study of Torah—to the way the ancient Israelites practiced their faith, centered on the Temple, priesthood, and sacrifice.

We concluded that celibacy in the Catholic Church is both biblical and authentically Jewish.

## QUESTIONS

1. Was celibacy practiced in the Old Testament? If so, by whom?
2. Who were the Essenes?
3. What evidence is there that the Essenes practiced celibacy? Did any other ancient groups practice celibacy?
4. Where is a theology of celibacy evident in the Old Testament?
5. Explain the notion of "perfect holiness" and what it would have meant to the Essenes.
6. What connection did the early Church see between the temple nature of the community and sexual behavior?

7. What does St. Paul teach about celibacy?

8. How early in the life of the Church was celibacy the dominant lifestyle for priests?

9. What is the relationship between celibacy and prophethood?

10. Contrast the religion of ancient Judaism with modern Judaism.

# Epilogue

Is the Catholic priesthood "biblical"? That was one of the questions we took up at the beginning of this book, and we are now in a position, I hope, to answer it definitively and positively: Yes, the priesthood of the Catholic Church, both the common or royal and the ministerial, is grounded in the texts of divine Revelation and the words and actions of Jesus in his earthly ministry.

A recovery of the Catholic teaching on priesthood is urgently needed in our own day, both among the laity and the clergy. First of all, we laity need to recover a sense of our priestly status—and that this status is not a lot of talk and theory, but something that makes a difference in how we live our daily lives. Too often we fall into a "clericalist" mindset—a view of the Church and reality that exaggerates the role of the ministerial priests. We expect priests to be religious professionals who "do the work of the Church" while we just pay our dues to the organization. Oftentimes, growth in the spiritual life, and taking our faith more seriously, is almost identified with "getting more active" in the parish and taking on more para-clerical roles, like lectoring or serving as an extraordinary minister of communion. While some are called to these roles, they should not be seen as an expression of the royal priesthood of the faithful, whose proper function is to *sanctify the temporal order*, not assist in the liturgy. *Sanctifying the temporal order* is quite a mouthful, but it means, basically, making the secular world a holier place: our office, worksite, classroom, and home—wherever it is that we live and work and fulfill our vocation. That is an "outward" looking perspective on the Christian life, not an "inward" one. Advancing in holiness goes hand in hand with moving out into the world, spreading the influence of the kingdom, rather than heading further inside the institutional Church. And a simple glance at the news sites make glaringly clear that we are in critical need of truly *priestly* Catholics in the media, business, medicine, politics, academia, as well as in the businesses, schools and services that make up the fabric of our everyday lives. The best way to begin is to start being those "priestly Catholics" ourselves: getting up every morning by offering our day to God by explicit act of prayer, then tackling each task as an opportunity to make it into an offering to God, by doing it with excellence while drawing on God's grace. So much more can be said on this, but some saints and spiritual writers—notably St. Josemaría Escrivá—have already spent their lives working out the implications of the common priesthood for the daily life of Catholics, and their books are readily available.

No less urgent is a recovery of strong priestly identity among our ministerial priests, our spiritual fathers. As I write this, the nation has been gripped with weeks of violence in our major cities, violence ostensibly provoked by the dismal social and economic conditions of our urban communities. Many solutions are bandied about by pundits and politicians, but only a few, quiet, marginalized voices dare to point out the condition that has perhaps the strongest statistical claim to be responsible for the conditions giving rise to the protests: *fatherlessness in our homes.* Sadly, this is a problem not limited to urban America, but rapidly growing in other areas and demographics. American culture—and many other modern societies—is suffering the devastating grief of *father absence*, which leads to so many pathologies: social, psychological, and spiritual.

We moderns are crying out in pain for a loving father in our lives. And in the contemporary situation, I am once again impressed by how God gifts his Church with the answers to the world's ills. The backbone of the Church is made up of an army of spiritual fathers—for fathers are what priests are in their deepest nature, fathers who image the love of God the Father toward their brothers and sisters on earth. Since becoming Catholic, I've been blessed with so many spiritual fathers in my life, who've helped me cope with the pain of life, experience God's love and forgiveness, and gather the courage to face obstacles on pilgrimage of this life. I've also been impressed at how effective the culture of priesthood within the Church is in delivering spiritual care: as a Catholic, I can approach a complete stranger in a foreign country on the other side of the world, and because he is a Catholic priest, within moments I can be unburdening myself of pain in the deepest recesses of my soul and receiving the forgiveness and guidance of a loving Father God through the voice of this man. How we need more men to take up this selfless vocation to be the image and likeness of God the Father toward His children on earth! If this book brings some encouragement to those who have accepted this vocation, and perhaps prompts some other young men to take it up, it will have fulfilled its purpose.